PRIVATE BUSINESS AND ECONOMIC REFORM IN CHINA

The revival of the "individual economy" in China in the late 1970s was justified on the grounds that it was economically appropriate and that it would be easily constrained by government regulation and by its dependence on socialist economy. Through the 1980s, however, reforms which decentralized economic power and increased the role of the profit motive dramatically weakened these limits. When state regulations conflicted with economic incentives, local officials often found informal solutions to the problem. While the private sector remained dependent on personal goodwill and informal relationships, it also developed rapidly and became a significant feature of the economy; one that was largely under local rather than central control. Thus the reforms have given rise to new interest networks, with which the private sector is intimately involved, and which are now fighting to preserve the benefits they have obtained from the reforms and to bend central policies to their own ends.

Based on Party and state documents, Chinese newspaper reports and surveys, the Chinese and Western scholarly literature and the author's own fieldwork, this important study examines the private sector as a case study of the mechanics of reform in China, emphasizing the relationships among local officials, private businesses, and central policy. The book traces the growth of private business in China since 1978 and focuses on the interaction between private sector policy and other reforms and examines how this has affected China's political economy.

Studies on Contemporary China

Studies on Contemporary China

PRIVATE BUSINESS AND ECONOMIC REFORM IN CHINA

SUSAN YOUNG

An East Gate Book

M.E. Sharpe
Armonk, New York
London, England

An East Gate Book

Permission has been granted for passages appearing in this book from the following sources:

Susan Young, "Wealth but Not Security: Attitudes toward Private Business in
the 1980s," in Andrew Watson, ed., *Economic Reform and Social Change in China*,
pp. 63–87. London: Routledge, 1992.

Susan Young, "Policy, Practice, and the Private Sector in China."
The Australian Journal of Chinese Affairs, no. 21, January 1989, pp. 57–80.

Susan Young, Wealth but Not Security: Attitudes toward Private Business in
the 1980s," *The Australian Journal of Chinese Affairs*,
no. 25, January 1991, pp. 115–139.

The first two sections of chapter 6, and the beginning of the section in chapter 7 on
"The New Approach to Central Control: 1989 and After," draw extensively on
Susan Young, "Private Entrepreneurs and Evolutionary Change in China," in
David S. G. Goodman and Beverley Hooper, eds., *China's Quiet Revolution: New
Institutions Between State and Society*. Melbourne: Longman Cheshire, 1994,
pp. 105–125. Permission of the publishers gratefully acknowledged.

Library of Congress Cataloging-in-Publication Data

Young, Susan, 1964–
Private business and economic reform in China / Susan Young.
p. cm. — (Studies on contemporary China)
"An east gate book."
Originally presented as the author's thesis (Ph.D.—University of Adelaide), 1991.
Includes bibliographical references and index.
ISBN 1-56324-500-0. — ISBN 1-56324-501-9 (pbk.)
1. Privatization—China. 2. Free enterprise—China. 3. Industrial policy—China.
4. China—Economic policy—1976- .I. Title. II. Series.
HD4318.Y68 1995
338.951—dc20
94-32541
CIP

Printed in the United States of America

The paper used in this publication meets the minimum requirements of
American National Standard for Information Sciences—
Permanence of Paper for Printed Library Materials,
ANSI Z 39.48-1984.

BM (c) 10   9   8   7   6   5   4   3   2   1
BM (p) 10   9   8   7   6   5   4   3   2   1

Contents

Acknowledgments

The bulk of the research for this book was done in preparation for a Ph.D. dissertation, submitted to the University of Adelaide in 1991. Fieldwork was funded by the University of Adelaide, the Australia–China Council, and the Federation of University Women–South Australia Inc. Further research was undertaken while I was teaching at the Centre for Asian Studies, University of Adelaide, with funding from the University and the Australian Academies of Social Sciences and Humanities–Chinese Academy of Social Sciences exchange program. I am grateful to these organizations for their support and to the Centre for Asian Studies for providing me with a pleasant and stimulating working environment.

While at Adelaide I was very fortunate to have been a student and colleague of Andrew Watson's, and much of what is good in this book is due to his help. I also gained a lot from discussions with colleagues in the Chinese Economy Research Unit, particularly Christopher Findlay and Li Qingzeng. Jonathan Unger and the anonymous readers of two papers I submitted to the *Australian Journal of Chinese Affairs* made comments and suggestions that raised issues not only for those papers but for my work as a whole. I am grateful to Ole Odgaard for the insights I have gained both from reading his work and from his helpful comments on several chapters of the original dissertation. I hasten to add, however, that none of these people is responsible for any errors in this book.

In China, I was given a great deal of help by Zhu Qingfang and Hu Xiaochun at the Institute of Sociology at the Chinese Academy of Social Sciences in Beijing, by Wang Shihua, Shen

Yi, Liu Jinshi, and, especially, Yang Gang at the Sichuan Academy of Social Sciences, by Xu Long at the Guangdong Academy of Social Sciences, and by numerous others who took time to arrange interviews for me or to talk to me themselves. I am very grateful to the Chengdu College of Geology for its hospitality whenever I have visited China and in particular to the late Dong Yibao and his wife, Yao Suzhu, for all their help and friendship over the years.

In the final stages of manuscript preparation I had to move to Denmark. Suddenly I had no office, no desk, no telephone, no printer, no library card—just an antique computer and a deadline. Without the wonderful welcome and generosity of the University of Copenhagen's Center for East and South-East Asian Studies, that deadline would have been extremely difficult to meet.

I am very grateful to John and Ruth Young for all their encouragement and for practical help like taking my first baby for Very Long Walks while I was writing. At that time, I was asked for ideas on what would make it easier for women to combine research and having children. The usual things like good childcare and bulk supplies of coffee sprang to mind, but the only really important thing I could think of, in the end, was that they should have husbands like Zhou Shaohua. Two more children later, I still feel the same way.

List of Abbreviations

CCP   Chinese Communist Party

FBZ, F51   Zhongguo renmin daxue shubao ziliao zhongxin, eds., *Fuyin baokan ziliao, F51, shangye jingji, shangye qiye guanli* (Reprints from newspapers and periodicals, F51, commercial economy and commercial enterprise administration)

FBZ, F22   Zhongguo renmin daxue shubao ziliao zhongxin, eds., *Fuyin baokan ziliao, F22, nongcun qiye guanli* (Reprints from newspapers and periodicals, F22, rural enterprise administration)

GMRB   *Guangming ribao* (Enlightenment Daily)

ICB   Bureau of Industry and Commerce (Gongshang xingzheng guanli ju)

ILA   Individual Laborers' Association (geti laodongzhe xiehui)

JJCK   *Jingji cankao* (Economic Information)

JJRB   *Jingji ribao* (Economic Daily)

NMRB   *Nongmin ribao* (Peasants' Daily)

RMRB   *Renmin ribao* (People's Daily)

SWB	British Broadcasting Corporation, *Summary of World Broadcasts: Part 3—The Far East*
ZGGSB	*Zhongguo gongshang bao* (Chinese Industry and Commerce)
ZTN	*Zhongguo tongji nianjian* (Statistical Yearbook of China)
ZXQN	*Zhongguo xiangzhen qiye nianjian* (China Township Enterprise Yearbook)

PRIVATE BUSINESS
AND
ECONOMIC
REFORM
IN CHINA

1

Introduction

After thirty years of "building socialism," China's leaders decided after the death of Mao Zedong that they had been building it the wrong way. Those who took over after the end of the Cultural Revolution were disenchanted with the existing cumbersome economic structure and volatile system of leadership and embarked on a course of reform aimed at revitalizing the economy, raising productivity, and delivering a rise in living standards that would prove the superiority of socialism. In spite of some disagreement among China's leaders over the extent to which the central planning system should be modified, the reforms took the course of increasing individual and local initiative and the power to act on it by transferring some economic functions from the bureaucracy to market forces and increasing the role of the profit motive in economic decision-making. This was a gradual process of experimentation, rather than a sudden switch to a completely new program, but one reform led to another until, by the 1990s, the result had moved far beyond the limited horizons envisioned in 1978.

The development of private business under the reforms clearly illustrates how this process evolved. Greatly reduced after collectivization in the mid-1950s and virtually eradicated during the Cultural Revolution, private business was revived as a quick, easy, and cheap way of alleviating some of the problems of the day: a sluggish economy with inadequate circulation of goods, failure to provide sufficient consumer goods and services to the public, and unemployment. Active encouragement of private business was a major policy shift for the Chinese Communist Party (CCP), which had formerly seen it as a remnant of capitalist society with the potential to engender capitalism of itself. It was something that should be rapidly phased out under socialism. Clearly some sections of the leadership still had grave doubts about the suitability of private business for socialist development, and the reformists took pains to assure them that under China's now firmly established system of public ownership, a small private economy would not lead to exploitation, inequality, and capitalism because it would be limited by the dominant publicly owned economy and government regulation.

Yet the revival of private business did not take place in isolation: it was part of a complex range of reforms, which began to alter profoundly the very economic and administrative structure that was supposed to limit it. The major reasons for the leadership's initial support of private business—the need to improve supplies of consumer goods and to provide jobs for peasants released from agriculture by the rural reforms, for urban residents returning from the countryside after the Cultural Revolution, and for new school leavers—became, if anything, more pressing as reforms took effect. This spurred reformists to overcome opposition and persist in encouraging private business. Meanwhile, as the rural economy opened up, and as market forces and the profit motive began to play an increasing role in the cities, too, opportunities for private business increased and its position became more secure. Above all, the reformist ideology stressed economic performance—in terms of increased output and profitability, increasing employment, and rising standards of living—as the main criterion of administrative or managerial success. In this atmosphere, many obstacles to the growth of private business gave way.

Growth and Scope of the Private Sector

This study does not deal with all forms of private economic activity in China, but focuses on businesses that are acknowledged to be private: mainly the sector of privately owned, profit-seeking, full-time businesses known as *geti gongshanghu*, or *getihu* (individual businesses), or the larger *siying qiye* (private enterprises). *Getihu* are officially defined as individually owned businesses employing up to eight people, including the owner but often discounting family members. *Siying qiye* are businesses with eight or more employees, owned by individuals, partners, or groups of up to thirty shareholders. Both kinds of business are predominantly engaged in retailing, catering, services, repairs, construction, transport, and light manufacturing. Agriculture is not included in this study, nor, in general, is the rural sideline economy, although the distinctions between specialized rural households (*zhuanyehu*), joint enterprises or partnerships (*lianheti*), and *getihu* or *siying qiye* are often blurred and the categories overlap. This trend increased in the latter half of the 1980s as there was increasing cooperation across ownership lines and the old categories began to be superseded.

When the reforms first began, only *getihu* were officially allowed, because of the need to avoid exploitation. According to Chinese sources, the limit of seven employees was derived from passages in *Capital* where Marx discusses the need for a certain number of people to be employed before the employer can accumulate capital. Marx gives one purely hypothetical example in which the employer has to employ eight people in order to extract enough surplus value to make twice the income of the employees, plus the same again to use as capital.[1] Although private enterprises quickly exceeded this limit and eventually obtained official acceptance, the issue of their political nature was an important one, and the division between *getihu* and *siying qiye* has had a significant impact on the development of private business under the reforms. Private business developed well beyond the marginal, stop-gap role outlined for it in 1978–81, both in its share of economic activity and in the size of enterprises, but the lack of an ideological justification for this growth meant that much of it was hidden or disguised, resulting in complex administrative problems.

Table 1.1

Recorded Private Businesses, 1981–1993 (year-end figures)

Year	Getihu	Siying qiye	Geti qiye in townships and villages
1981	1,827,752		
1982	2,614,006		
1983	5,901,032		
1984	9,329,464		3,295,900
1985	11,712,560		9,253,500
1986	12,111,560		12,332,000
1987	13,725,746		14,730,700
1988	14,526,931		16,091,700
1989	12,471,937	90,581	16,081,200
1990	13,281,974	98,141	16,071,700
1991	14,145,000	108,000	16,788,500
1992	15,339,200	139,600	18,487,200
1993	15,483,000	184,000	

Sources: 1981–90: Guojia gongshang xingzheng guanliju xinxi zhongxin, eds., *Zhongguo gongshang xingzheng tongji sishi nian* (Forty Years of Statistics on Chinese Industrial and Commercial Administration), pp. 164, 158–59. 1991: *Zhongguo gongshang bao* (Chinese Industry and Commerce), 17 February 1992, p. 3. 1992: *Zhongguo tongji nianjian* (Statistical Yearbook of China), 1993, pp. 113–14. 1993: Interview, ICB, Beijing, December 1993.

Note: Numbers of *getihu* and *siying qiye* are based on Bureau of Industry and Commerce figures. Numbers of *geti qiye* in townships and villages are based on Ministry of Agriculture figures (source: *Zhongguo xiangzhen qiye nianjian* [Chinese Township Industries Yearbook], 1993, p. 147). The two sets of figures are not mutually exclusive.

Most of the official reports and policy discussions on the private sector in China use statistics from the State Statistical Bureau or the state Bureau of Industry and Commerce (ICB), a bureau set up directly under the State Council to administer business activity under the reforms. These figures present the private sector as fairly small, both because they compare it with the huge urban state sector and because they are urban-based and have not yet managed to reach down to include all rural private businesses. Even so, the figures are impressive for a sector that was virtually nonexistent (only 150,000 private businesses were recorded in 1978) when the reforms began. By late 1993, there were over 15.6 million *getihu* and *siying qiye* registered with the ICB (see Table 1.1). In 1991 *getihu* made up 79 percent of industrial enterprises, although since most were very small they only produced 5.7 percent of gross industrial output value.[2] In the same year *getihu* made up nearly 86 percent of retail, service, and food service outlets in China[3] and 19.6 percent of retail sales volume.[4]

A significant division emerged in the nature and role of the urban and rural private sectors. In the cities, private businesses clustered in the small-scale retail, service, or food service industries, which enhanced the impact of private businesses on public life and public opinion, but was also the reason for the popular, critical image of the *getihu* as being engaged in these essentially nonproductive trades. Contrary to this popular image as presented in the media, over 75 percent of private businesses actually developed in rural areas, after reforms promoted a surge in rural enterprise growth (see Figure 1.1). Of these nearly 40 percent were engaged in manufacturing or processing industries. The private sector has played an important role in the development of township enterprises (*xiangzhen qiye*): indeed, the statistics recorded by the Ministry of Agriculture for these (mainly rural) enterprises alone include many more private businesses than are listed by the ICB for both rural and urban enterprises. These figures show 18.48 million private businesses (*geti qiye*, used for private businesses of any size) in townships and villages by the end of 1992, making up 88.4 percent of township enterprises and providing 44 percent of jobs.[5] The private share of the gross output value of township enterprises rose from 6.9 percent in 1984, when figures were first released, to 27 percent in 1992.[6]

It should be borne in mind that both the urban and rural figures list only those businesses formally acknowledged to be privately owned. In some localities many "village-run" and joint enterprises are in fact privately owned. The proportions vary widely from place to place. In some Sichuan townships visited by the author it was obvious that nearly all joint enterprises were private, and local businesspeople estimated that the same could be said of about 50 percent of the village-run enterprises; each locality chooses its own ownership strategy, however, so other researchers have found

Figure 1.1 **Recorded Private Businesses** (year-end)

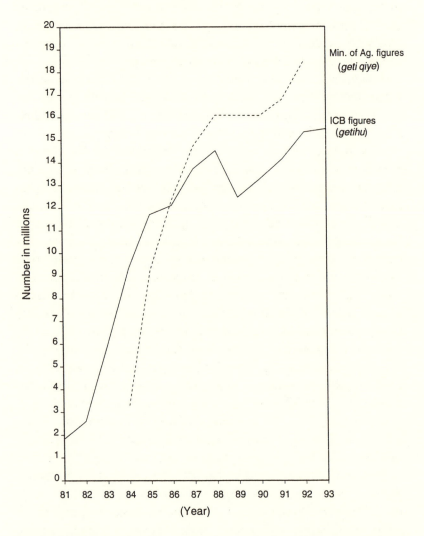

much stronger collective control elsewhere.[7] This issue of regional variation is one that is clearly very important for a full understanding of the development of the Chinese private sector, but because the effective ownership and management of an enterprise can be very different from its registration, it will require extensive fieldwork by many researchers to explore it fully. In addition to differences arising from local conditions and local administrative approaches, the private sector has followed the Chinese economy as a whole in developing much faster in the east than the west, the proportions in 1993 being approximately 5:3:2 from eastern to central to western China for numbers of *getihu*, and 7:2:1 for *siying qiye*.[8]

The Private Sector and Reform

The importance of the private sector in China is only partly related to its size. A major concern has, of course, been the ideological impact of a thriving private sector whose growth rate has far outpaced that of the socialist sectors. China's economic reforms have handed an increasing share of economic decision-making to those at lower levels—managers or local government owners of state and collective enterprises, and the local levels of state administrative organs—who have often responded to market pressures by cooperating with private enterprise. Thus the private sector has become increasingly intertwined with other ownership sectors and with local government, in ways that have then further influenced the direction of economic change in China. Some of the most important aspects of this integration resulted from reforms to the organization of state and collective enterprises, such as contracting or leasing to individuals, joint-stock ownership of enterprises, and increased linkages among enterprises as the planning system was cut back, which continued to open up more opportunities for private enterprise. The new power relationships emerging from this situation, particularly in rural areas, were important not only for the future of private enterprise in China but also for the kind of society and economy to develop from the reforms.

Many of the opportunities for growth in the private sector arose from the way in which new policies were developed and put into effect. The method of reform used after 1978 was a hands-on approach in which local levels were asked or allowed to try out new practices first, before the results were evaluated and confirmed in official central policies. The detailed formulation of regulations and administrative procedures to match new practices came last of all, only after these practices had proved themselves and gained some degree of support. This was advantageous in that official policies and regulations could be made on the basis of some knowledge of real conditions, and in that it enabled reformers to push changes through without first completing the long process of establishing their ideological credentials. But it also created administrative problems.

To begin with, the reforms gave local authorities wide discretionary powers. This meant that they could choose either to promote reform or to stifle it. The incentives introduced by fiscal contracting and other measures equating good performance with industrial and commercial development meant that on the whole they tended to support it, but they also manipulated it in ways that did not always suit the central government. Furthermore, such a reform process made it difficult to keep track of changes in the structure of economic organization and regulate them effectively: administrators were placed in the difficult position of trying to fit a wide range of situations into a limited and outdated range of categories. Finally, reliance on the discretion of local authorities made private entrepreneurs extremely reliant on personal connections. Coupled with the hybrid market–plan economy created by the reforms, this made the private sector a fertile breeding ground for corruption.

On another level, this pattern of reform also created a wide gap between ideology and practice, putting the leadership in an ultimately untenable position. As a result the 1980s were marked by major debates concerning issues such as the optimal combination of plan and market, how to stimulate initiative without losing control of the economy, inequality and exploitation under socialism, and the nature and proper distribution of ownership. The rapid growth of the private sector was closely related to all these issues, not least because it presented a fundamental challenge to orthodox CCP ideology. The more radical protagonists in the debate claimed that it was precisely those reforms in the state sector that came closest to privatization, such as leasing and contracting, which had shown the best economic results. Yet China was still led by a communist party, which saw public ownership of the means of production and government direction of the economy as key determinants of socialism.

As a Chinese scholar remarked in 1980, a train running along two such divergent paths was bound to be derailed sooner or later.[9] The conservative revival marked by the repression of the protest movement in June 1989 appeared at first to be just such a derailing of the reforms. In particular it halted the ownership debate and inspired a new determination to limit the private sector. Yet almost as soon as the attack on private business was launched, concern at unemployment and the depressed market—in addition to local resistance—caused central leaders to reconsider. By the end of the 1980s the private sector had been re-established as an integral and significant part of the Chinese economy.

This study is a history of this re-emergence of private enterprise in China and seeks to explain it in terms of the economic and political processes set in train by the reforms of the 1980s. It is based primarily on the Chinese popular and academic press and on interviews undertaken on visits to China in 1988, 1991, 1992, and 1993. Interviewees included scholars, officials from relevant departments and local governments, and some sixty private business operators. The majority of the interviews were conducted over eight weeks in 1988 and three weeks in 1992. Most enterprises visited were in the Sichuan cities of Chengdu and Zigong and the counties of Xindu, Dazu, and Anyue, with shorter visits to Beijing and Guangzhou. Most interviewees were introduced through the Chinese Academy of Social Sciences, and interviews were conducted in the company of observers; a small number were arranged privately by friends in Chengdu.

The private sector, being relatively independent, market-led, competitive, unstable, and inegalitarian, epitomizes everything old-style Communists most distrust about the reforms as a whole; and yet they admit it is useful. Because of the unusual opportunities arising from the reform process, the Chinese private sector has become so entrenched that it would be difficult and very costly to repress. Yet at the same time the means by which it attained this position are such that it remains vulnerable and politically suspect. It is also relatively easily influenced by the local-level officials who have given it room to develop. Their actions not only make it more difficult to exert central control but also influence the way private business evolves. This mirrors the problems faced by China's leaders across the whole range of reforms as China seeks to establish a basis for sustained, stable growth and development. A study of the private sector, therefore, provides a way of looking at the process of reform, and how this process has affected the outcome, not only for private business but for the course of development in China.

Notes

1. Karl Marx, *Capital*, Vol. 1, pp. 291–92.
2. Guojia tongji ju, eds., *Zhongguo tongji nianjian* (Statistical Yearbook of China, hereafter *ZTN*), 1992, p. 403.
3. Ibid., p. 584.
4. Ibid., p. 26.
5. *Zhongguo xiangzhen qiye nianjian* editorial committee, eds., *Zhongguo xiangzhen qiye nianjian* (Township Enterprise Yearbook, hereafter *ZXQN*), 1993, pp. 145–46.
6. Ibid., p. 147.
7. For example, Jean C. Oi, "The Fate of the Collective after the Commune," and the studies in William A. Byrd and Lin Qingsong, eds., *China's Rural Industry*.
8. Interview, State ICB, Beijing, December 1993.
9. Li Honglin, former president of the Fujian Academy of Social Sciences, quoted in *Shanghai shijie bao* (Shanghai World News), 11 April 1988. See British Broadcasting Corporation, *Summary of World Broadcasts, Part 3—The Far East* [hereafter *SWB*], 30 April 1988, FE/0139 B2/2–3.

—————— 2 ——————

Reviving Private Industry and Commerce

Although the revival of the private business sector became an integral part of China's economic reforms, it was consistently presented as peripheral. From the earliest stages of the rural reforms private business played a vital role by providing an alternative to agricultural employment, utilizing small-scale investment, stimulating commodity exchange, and building up the marketing networks that were a necessary adjunct to the household responsibility system which gave each family the power to make its own production and marketing decisions. In the cities private traders were important in improving supplies of agricultural produce to urban residents, improving supplies of consumer goods and services in general, and providing new employment opportunities. Yet the private sector was presented as peripheral because of all the reform measures it was one of the least acceptable politically. For almost thirty years after taking power, the CCP had worked to reduce the role of private enterprise in the Chinese economy, with the aim of eventually eradicating it. To turn around and promote it, therefore, was a major change that conflicted sharply with past ideology.

Accordingly, the promotion of private business was first introduced discreetly and without fanfare and gradually worked into the framework of official policy as reformers and reformist ideas strengthened their position in the party leadership. The theoretical debate that accompanied these developments followed a similar course, presenting itself less as an academic search for truth than as a political search for justification. This reformist sleight of hand was to prove a double-edged sword. While it facilitated the introduction of controversial measures, it meant that important administrative and political issues remained unsolved. In time this led to serious discrepancies in theory, policy, and practice, which themselves became barriers to further reform. In 1978, though, the main task for reformers was to get the first policy changes off the ground. This chapter examines how they did this for private business.

The New Policy of Promoting Private Business

As with most of the reforms, the Third Plenum of the CCP's Eleventh Central Committee in December 1978 is seen as marking the beginning of the official revival of private business. In fact the beginnings of the policy can be traced back to the loosening of market restrictions that followed Zhou Enlai's Four Modernizations proposal of 1975, the details of which were worked out by Deng Xiaoping.[1] Even as early as 1976, some areas began to allow new private businesses. In Tianjin, for example, the number of private businesses rose by over two thousand during 1976–78, largely as a means of providing jobs for people returning to the city from the countryside.[2] At the time, the legal position of private business, as set down in the constitution of 1975 and also in 1978, was that of a marginal sector to be tolerated temporarily and tightly controlled:

> The state may allow nonagricultural individual labor involving no exploitation of others, within the limits prescribed by law and under unified arrangement by neighborhood organizations in cities and towns or by production teams in rural people's communes. At the same time, these individual laborers should be guided onto the road of socialist collectivization step by step.[3]

The Third Plenum itself made no specific announcements concerning private business, but it signified the official adoption of economic modernization and growth as the paramount concern of the CCP and of the view that the way to achieve such development was not ideological education but economic incentive and technological improvements.

Significantly, Chen Yun was made a member of the Politburo and a vice chairman of the Central Committee. Although he was on the conservative side of reform, and came to be seen as an archconservative planophile by 1989, he had never had anything against a limited amount of free enterprise and had been in the camp that revived it in the early 1960s. Indeed, private sector policy in the late 1970s and early 1980s was very much in line with Chen's earlier ideas, seeing a limited amount of private business as useful in taking on tasks of small-scale production and distribution that were difficult for the planning system to perform effectively.[4] The Third Plenum's emphasis on economic development and individualistic incentives also gave impetus to the revival of private business. Once this had occurred, local governments began to formulate procedures for the administration of the individual economy, which was already developing by this time. In early 1979 the State Council ratified the growth of free markets by issuing Document No. 102 on improving administration in urban and rural markets, and the licensing of individual peddlers was one response to this document.[5] An official in the Sichuan ICB told me that the bureau's first move was to go around issuing licenses to those people who had already been operating private businesses for some time.

At this early stage, individual businesses were still heavily restricted. In general only those without other options, such as former *getihu* who had been put out of business in the Cultural Revolution, were eligible for licensing; although one of the reasons for promoting the individual economy was to increase employment opportunities, local governments preferred to channel young job-seekers into collective or cooperative employment.[6] *Getihu* were also restricted, at least in theory, to very simple handicraft, hawking, and repair businesses, as it was felt that they should not be allowed to compete with the state and collective sectors. These restrictions, however, were progressively re-moved. In particular, a national work conference on employment sponsored by the Central Committee in August 1980 gave new impetus to the growth of the private sector and was followed by other central initiatives such as provision for bank loans to *getihu* and lowering *getihu* taxes.[7] With these developments, the growth of private business became widespread and was no longer con-fined to a few experimental areas, and provincial governments issued a series of regulations on the administration of the individ-ual economy at this time.[8] Yet the individual economy still had an experimental flavor, and was confirmed only by a set of State Council regulations on the urban, nonagricultural individual economy in July 1981.[9]

This sequence of unpublicized experimentation, followed by a general "in principle" approval, then by ratification and specific regulations only after the reform in question is well established, crops up time and time again in the development of the private sector in China. The 1981 regulations in effect gave the stamp of approval to the already flourishing private sector, and subsequent regulations also followed this pattern, approving new develop-ments in private business after they had already occurred. This common pattern for the introduction of controversial reforms is useful to reformists because it enables them to bypass the formal ideological debate required for public, legislative sanction of a reform and, in turn, use the successful results of the reform as ammunition in the debate.

The 1981 regulations allowed the nonagricultural individual economy (*geti jingji*) as a supplement to the state and collective sectors. Individuals were allowed to engage in "all kinds of small-scale handicrafts, retail commerce, catering, services, re-pairs, nonmechanized transport and building repairs," which were beneficial to the national economy and did not involve the exploitation of others. The regulations promised that the state would protect the rights and interests of private operators, but also imposed certain limits on their size and fields of operation. Only unemployed youths or retirees with certain skills to pass on were allowed by the regulations to engage in individual business; this new focus was the result of the employment initiatives since the August 1980 employment conference. Individual businesses were allowed to employ others, but were limited to up to two assistants and no more than five apprentices, and were only allowed to used nonmechanized tools and vehicles. In fact individual businesses had already developed beyond these limits (for example, by exceeding the employment limits, or by obtaining supplies from other than official channels) by the time the regulations were released.[10] The limits were there more for political purposes, to signal the official role of the individual economy as a limited sector of small businesses, well under the control of the socialist state and therefore unlikely to develop any capitalist tendencies.

The 1981 regulations dealt specifically only with urban businesses, but were to apply in principle to rural ventures also. Private businesses (some already beyond the *getihu* employment limit) were also developing in rural areas, and the 1982 constitution acknowledged the urban and rural individual economy. It was not until February 1984, however, that a set of regulations for rural individual enterprises was passed.[11] The development of policy toward the rural private sector is another example of the underhand pattern of development of reform measures, one with important implications for the way in which rural reform was represented and perceived. Until the rural economy became more commercialized, the course of rural reform meant that there was no need for specific procedures governing the administration of individual enterprises; indeed the diversity of rural reforms meant that unified national regulations would have been inappropriate. Under the rural reforms, production teams contracted land and specific tasks in a variety of forms of contract responsibility system. This evolved into a virtual privatization of agriculture in which economic management devolved to households. Some households then specialized in nonagricultural activities and became the "specialized households" (*zhuanyehu*), many of which were, in effect, private nonagricultural businesses. Hence private businesses were often able to develop in rural areas without the need for guidelines or regulations specifically dealing with them as such. The justification for this lay in the nature of rural organization, based on the commune system. Until the collapse of the communes, peasants running *zhuanyehu* were still considered part of this system, one in which the basic means of production—the land—was still collectively owned. The origin of the *zhuanyehu* within the collective agricultural economy thus meant that their private nature could be ignored and they could be dealt with as "a management level within the cooperative economy,"[12] rather than as an independent private sector. It was only the urban private businesses, and those in rural areas that became undeniably separated from the collective as the rural economy became more diverse and commercialized—whose operators, for example, were no longer involved in agriculture at all—which had to be acknowledged as private businesses. Some of these businesses appeared as rural individual businesses (*getihu*) in the ICB's statistics beginning in 1981.[13]

Here again a wide gap developed between the official version of events and actual practice. Where necessary, administrative practices acknowledged the similarity between *getihu* and *zhuanyehu*; and many manuals on business administration dealt with both categories together.[14] Regulations concerning questions such as supplies to individuals, private transport of goods, and market prices usually applied to the activities themselves and did not distinguish between *getihu, zhuanyehu*, or indeed cooperative enterprises. *Zhuanyehu* were not, however, generally registered as *getihu*. This meant that they did not have to be included in policy debates on the degree of development of private enterprise. The exclusion of *zhuanyehu* from statistics on the individual economy also enabled many discussions of rural private industry and commerce to present it as much smaller than would otherwise have been possible.

The origin of the *zhuanyehu* within the collective system meant that they could be seen as socialist in nature and therefore not a problem ideologically. The same was even more true of agriculture, as peasants did still have strong contractual links with the collective. Partnerships or enterprises run by several families, the *lianhu* or *lianheti*, could also be seen as cooperative rather than private. The acknowledged private sector of *getihu* and, later, *siying qiye*, however, presented much more of a problem politically as it had to be accommodated within party policy and ideology. Therefore the policy of encouraging the recognized private economy, its implementation, and the debates surrounding it, are the focus of this book. Parallel to the growth of the urban and rural "individual economy," however, an increasingly complex range of reforms were taking place in agriculture, rural industry and commerce, and eventually urban enterprises as well. These led to the further reassessment and reorganization of ownership taking place in the 1990s, which is providing new opportunities for private entrepreneurs.

The Case for Private Business: 1978–1983

Economic Motivation

The case in favor of reviving the individual economy rested on the reformist argument that the main task for China "in the current stage" was to promote the development of the productive forces. (In time, this argument was to be refined into the theory of the "initial stage of socialism" officially expounded by Zhao Ziyang at the Thirteenth Party Congress in 1987.)[15] It therefore followed that the development of the individual economy was justified at least until the productive forces were developed enough to make it easily replaceable. This really boiled down to saying that the individual economy should be developed as long as it was economically beneficial.

> The relations of production in any society are determined by the level of the productive forces. The uneven economic development in China requires a corresponding multilevel economic structure ranging from the state sector to the private sector.[16]

This theme in the debate was not intended as a slur on socialism, but emphasized the role of objective economic factors, such as the lack of mechanization and inadequate transport and storage, in determining the appropriateness or otherwise of a form of organization. "Our productive forces are low, transportation is inconvenient, and our production tools and transport facilities are backward," lamented *Renmin ribao* (People's Daily), apropos of advocating more individual businesses.[17] Many functions in the economy, particularly in China where production, distribution, and storage were not highly developed, were best performed on a small scale. In such circumstances no greater efficiencies could be gained from large-scale collective organization and centralized direction. The reformist position was that the virtual elimination of the individual economy and the reduced independence of collective enterprises (the idea being that state ownership was best, collective ownership a stepping-stone to state ownership, and individual ownership a remnant of the capitalist past) had been a mistake. Larger organizations simply had not provided an adequate replacement. What had often happened was that a number of small businesses were amalgamated into one big one. In Beijing, for example, while the population increased 300 percent from 1953 to 1978, the number of retail, catering, and service outlets fell by over 80 percent.[18] Many traditional products and services were simply no longer offered, as the central planning system was not well suited to diversity or catering to small markets. These arguments were not new, of course; they owed much to the economic debates of 1956–58 and the early 1960s. The critique of consumer services echoed Chen Yun's speeches of 1956 and 1961–62, and the leading proponents of reviving the individual economy in 1979–81 included Dong Fureng and He Jianzhang, who had been active in the 1960s search for an alternative model of socialist economics.[19] Of all the protagonists, Dong Fureng took the issue of collective versus private the furthest:

> Under certain circumstances, the sector of private ownership should be preserved and even developed within certain limits, for in many

respects, its functions *cannot be replaced* by either the ownership of the whole people or by collective ownership. For instance, repair shops, services, petty trades, and handicrafts can be run better by individuals than by the collective.[20]

The implication of most arguments made in favor of promoting the individual economy, however, was still that once the productive forces became more developed, large-scale, socialist organization would be more efficient and would replace the individual economy.[21] This was a very hard argument for those who opposed the individual economy as a source of capitalist regeneration to refute, as it accepted the assertion that socialized large-scale production was not just the inevitable trend as the productive forces became more developed, but superior to the individual economy. As the productive forces became more developed, socialist enterprises would simply outcompete individual businesses, which would disappear entirely with the arrival of communism.

Perhaps the most important economic rationale for promoting the individual economy (and, unofficially, larger private enterprises as well), was the need to increase employment opportunities. The rural reforms were bound to release some of the huge reservoir of surplus labor that had been tied to agriculture under the commune system. Rural townships and villages often lacked the resources to develop enough collective industry to employ this surplus. In urban areas, after the death of Mao Zedong and the fall of the "Gang of Four" faction in late 1976, many of the 17 million or so "educated youth" who had been sent to rural areas began to return.[22] There was also a residue of young people who had evaded being sent to the countryside, but who had no jobs. In addition, population growth in past years meant that jobs had to be found for some 3 to 5 million school leavers each year who were neither continuing their education nor entering the army.[23] By 1982, 7 million people were joining the job waiting lists per year.[24] Yet this was a time when economic growth had been slow and state enterprises were incapable of absorbing such large numbers of new employees. Many were in fact already overstaffed as a result of the CCP's previous commitment to full employment. Given these circumstances, there were strong incentives for governments at all levels to pursue any and all available employment alternatives.

The relative difficulty, speed, and cost of setting up individual businesses, as opposed to government-sponsored employment, was of great importance here. It was calculated in 1983 that the average cost of creating one job was over 10,000 (approximately $5,000 at the official rate) yuan in state heavy industry, over 6,000 yuan in state light industry, and around 3,000 yuan in a collective unit. In contrast, an individual business could be set up for a few hundred yuan, and of course the few hundred yuan would normally come not from the state but from private savings.[25] At a time when state resources were strained, and likely to become more so as fiscal reforms reduced the role of the central budget, this was a strong argument for promoting the individual economy. Individual businesses were also an easy solution in that they required no complicated infrastructure and were therefore quick to set up, and unlike collectives and many cooperatives they needed no umbrella organization to get them going. All that was required was for restrictions to be removed: individual incentive would do the rest. Accordingly, the national conference on labor and employment in August 1980 resolved that individually run businesses should be actively encouraged in order to increase employment opportunities. This provided further impetus to the early growth of the individual economy.[26]

Another important reason for the promotion of private business was simply to improve living standards by responding to consumer demand. Inadequate provision of consumer goods and services was a problem endemic to centrally planned economies, stemming both from investment priorities at the central level and from the incompatibility of numerous, varied, atomized goods and services with large-scale bureaucratic organization in conditions of limited storage, transport, and communications facilities. One of the goals of the post-Mao era has been to reverse this situation and improve consumer supplies. This was part of a switch in development strategy away from the concentration on heavy industry that had prevailed in spite of Mao's attempts to change it, toward light industries that were cheaper and quicker to develop.[27]

An emphasis on light industry and improving supplies to consumers does not, in itself, demand the promotion of private businesses. In the context of socialist development it is possible to imagine small cooperatives or collectives, which might have the same advantages of independence, adaptability, and incentives for good service and yet be more ideologically acceptable than individual ownership. Indeed in China small-scale cooperatives in light manufacturing, handicrafts and retail, service, and catering ventures were actively encouraged in the late 1970s, particularly as a way of providing jobs for urban youth. Many were started up under the ægis of street committees, following a pattern already well-established in the Cultural Revolution. Rural township governments were also seeking to encourage collective enterprises both to generate employment and to develop their local economies. Collective and cooperative enterprises, however, could not be so independent of bureaucracy as were individually owned businesses. They required organization and administration by government organizations or enterprises, and needed more start-up capital than an individually run business.[28] This was often highlighted in interviews in rural Sichuan in 1992: for example, a district enterprise office head explained how, when private business was first allowed, many families were already quietly doing business of one sort or another simply to survive: the collective system had not been adequately providing for them.[29]

Closely related to the issue of increasing the emphasis on light industry and consumer supplies was the reformers' desire to increase the "commoditization" of the economy; that is, to increase the proportion of goods distributed through market transactions rather than by bureaucratic allocation. It was argued that individual businesses would help to stimulate market activity and the circulation of commodities, both through their own efforts and by providing competition to stir state and collective units out of their notorious indifference to customers and sales figures. Like the suggestion that the low level of development of the productive forces demanded continued reliance on the individual economy in some spheres, this argument also rested partly on the underdeveloped state of China's transport and communications. Whereas large state and collective units dealt in bulk, which would require further investment before transport could be improved, private individuals would, if allowed to, carry small loads of goods from one place to another wherever there was a market for them. This was of particular importance in relation to rural reforms: as peasants were allowed to sell more of their produce on the free market, the amount being transported into the cities would rise and supplies to urban consumers would improve. Conversely, private hawkers were prepared to take small loads of manufactured goods —clothes, for example, or small everyday items—and travel around rural markets giving peasants something to buy with their rising incomes. The individual economy, therefore, would be extremely important to the success of the first major step in the reforms, the rural responsibility system.

Political Credentials

Having set out the economic arguments for reviving the individual economy, its supporters also had to make it acceptable politically, without challenging established parameters of socialism and the superiority of public ownership. They set about doing so with impressive mental agility, concentrating on rebutting fears that reviving the individual economy was a backward step that would lead to exploitation, inequality, and the restoration of capitalism.

The foundation of the pro–private business case was, of course, the productive forces argument, which served both to deny any denigration of the ultimate superiority of public ownership and to argue that the individual economy was not only harmless but actually beneficial to socialist development. If the achievement of full socialism was prevented by a lack of economic development, then it followed that socialism was best served by whatever promoted such development. If private ownership was shown to do this better than collective or state ownership in some trades or areas, then it should be allowed to continue. The CCP's June 1981 assessment of its history since 1949 rejected the past emphasis on the political or economic superiority of public ownership when it declared, "The reform and improvement of the socialist relations of production must be in accordance with the state of the forces of production, and be conducive to the development of production."[30]

The early debate, like early policy, was entirely in terms of the "individual economy," the *geti jingji*, involving, in accordance with the constitution, no exploitation. At this stage participants on all sides of the debate agreed that larger businesses, in which those who owned the means of production employed those who did not, were unacceptable under socialism. Indeed, many of the arguments in favor of the individual economy rested on smallness: both the small size of individual businesses and the smallness of the sector as a whole in relation to the publicly owned economy.[31] The individual economy was to act as a "supplement" to the state and collective sectors, "filling in the gaps" they left in the economy, particularly in the distribution of consumer goods and services and in employment. At first, even small private businesses were often mentioned in the same breath as collectives, apparently in an effort to slide them in unnoticed. "People who . . . feel that the collective economy is 'unsafe' and the individual economy is dangerous, are completely mistaken. You cannot put developing collective and individual economy on the same level as capitalism."[32] It was not at first proposed that individual businesses should be established in areas traditionally considered economically important; the individual economy was seen as appropriate only for sectors such as retailing, catering, consumer services, and handicrafts: "the trades, the state and collective economies don't do or don't do enough."[33]

Thus just as the early reform program as a whole sought to create a system in which market forces would be used to enliven the economy, without challenging the supremacy of central planning, the individual economy was proposed as a kind of economic plaster, which would cover up a few holes in the economy without changing its basic form. In fact, the private economy very quickly began to exceed the limits prescribed for it, injecting a certain unreality into the debate. Nevertheless, political constraints demanded that the fiction of the smallness and subordination of the private economy be maintained.

A key issue in the discussion was whether or not the individual economy was capitalist in nature or would lead to capitalism. Its supporters argued that it was not capitalist as it involved little or no exploitation. Although individual businesspeople were allowed to employ two assistants and up to five apprentices, they also participated in labor themselves, and the relationship between the assistants or apprentices and their employers was one of mutual assistance rather than exploitation. Under socialist conditions, these employees were also owners of the means of production through the system of public ownership, and this, in some unexplained manner, would prevent them from being exploited.[34] Notably, the argument very quickly shifted from the "no exploitation" of the constitution and early regulations to allowing for some exploitation, so long as the employer also participated in labor. An ICB cadre went so far as to say that since the employer's income was "only" two or three times the employees', this could not be called exploitation.[35] Once this step was made, it was only a matter of time before the employer's management decisions were counted as labor, in a line of argument that owed more to Smith than to Marx.[36] This type of argument was seldom seen in the early years, however, and became more common only after around 1985, in response to the developments such as individual leasing and private ownership of large enterprises. This was really a new stage in the debate concerning private enterprise and ownership reform, and will be discussed separately in chapter 7.

The case for the harmlessness of the individual economy rested not only on the internal relations of businesses but on their external environment. It was repeatedly argued that the individual economy could not lead to capitalism because socialism had been established in China and therefore the objective conditions for the development of capitalism—private ownership of the means of production, labor power as a commodity, and the opportunity to turn money into capital—did not exist.

An adjunct to this assertion was the argument that the individual economy could never dominate or significantly alter an economy, but had always, throughout history, been subordinate:

> The individual economy is a relatively ancient economic form. It began in the final stages of primitive society, passed through the different stages of social development of slave, feudal and capitalist society, and still exists in socialist society. But in each different society, the individual economy has not and cannot have a dominant position. It can only be subordinate to the dominant economic component of each society, and be influenced and restricted by it in development and role. The individual economy was subordinate to the slave economy in slave society, to the feudal economy in feudal society, to the capitalist economy in capitalist society, and therefore in today's socialist society, subordinate to the socialist publicly owned economy.[37]

This subordination, it was argued, found concrete expression in the control of the economy by government regulation and through the individual economy's dependence on the public sector for supplies.

> The small amount of individual economy that remains after socialist transformation is different from the individual economy before socialist transformation. . . . After the socialist transformation of the means of production, the individual economy is only a very small proportion of the national economy, and furthermore no longer has links with capitalist industry and commerce. . . . Under conditions in which the socialist publicly owned economy has overwhelming dominance, the individual economy is controlled by the socialist

publicly owned economy . . . and becomes a supplement to the socialist publicly owned economy. At the same time the individual economy relies on the socialist economy for supplies, loans, and marketing its products.[38]

This approach had the added advantage of being able to promote the individual economy for economic reasons, while not seriously criticizing the CCP's policy of socialist transformation in the 1950s, for it was precisely this transformation which had established a secure socialist state. Whereas in the past the individual economy may have tended to give rise to capitalism, conditions were now quite different.[39] "As long as socialist state ownership plays a dominant role in the economy, the existence and development of a sector of private ownership is not likely to breed capitalism."[40] Some of the more idealistic supporters of the individual economy even argued that after thirty years of socialist education, people themselves were more socialistic. Those who engaged in individual business did so not in order to develop capitalism, become unduly rich, or exploit others, but to make a contribution to their country and help the Four Modernizations.[41]

Conclusion

Until around 1984, the case for reviving the individual economy rested very much on the small size, simple technology, and limited scope of individual business. The way reformists continued doggedly along this theme, in the face of mounting evidence to the contrary, indicates continued opposition on the grounds that the individual economy would involve exploitation and inequality, be difficult to control, and even lead to a regeneration of capitalism. This opposition was rarely seen in the public debate, except in the continued reiteration of the pro–private business argument and statements that "some comrades" said that the individual economy was capitalist in nature. Meanwhile, the implementation of this reform and others was the responsibility of administrators at lower levels. It is here in the practice of reform that opposition to private businesses, and their precarious position in a system arranged around collective organizations, was most clearly manifested.

Notes

1. The policy documents that summed up the Zhou–Deng call for political stability and renewed emphasis on economic growth and technology-led modernization were promptly denounced by the Left as "three poisonous weeds," and Deng was ousted for the second time in April 1976. But provincial support for Deng's policies remained strong, causing a liberalization of local policies. See the discussion in John Gardner, *Chinese Politics and the Succession to Mao*, ch. 3.

2. Marcia Yudkin, *Making Good*, p. 22; Dorothy J. Solinger, *Chinese Business under Socialism*, p. 201.

3. The words "involving no exploitation of others" and the provision that individual laborers should be guided toward collectivization were dropped from the constitution in 1982. See Jill Barrett, "What's New in China's New Constitution?" p. 313.

4. See Chen's late 1950s speeches translated in Nicholas Lardy and Kenneth Lieberthal, eds., *Chen Yun's Strategy for China's Development*, and the introduction to the same volume.

5. For a meticulous account of the development of official policy toward the individual economy in 1978–83, based on a collection of key provincial and central documents, see Susan Muth, "Private Business under Socialism," ch. 3.

6. Ibid., p. 80; Chao Yü-shen, "Expansion of Individual Economy in Mainland China," p. 8.

7. Muth, "Private Business," pp. 81–82.

8. Ibid., pp. 85–86.

9. "Guowuyuan guanyu chengzhen fei nongye geti jingji ruogan zhengcexing guiding" (Certain policy regulations of the State Council on the urban nonagricultural individual economy), 7 July 1981, in *Siying he geti jingji shiyong fagui daquan*, pp. 61–64.

10. *Jingji cankao* (Economic Information, hereafter *JJCK*), 5 November 1987, p. 4; Yudkin, *Making Good*, p. 29.

11. "Guowuyuan guanyu nongcun geti gongshangye de ruogan guiding" (Certain regulations of the State Council on rural individual industry and commerce), 27 February 1984, published in *Renmin ribao* (People's Daily, hereafter *RMRB*), 12 March 1984.

12. Li Chengxun and Zhou Zhixiang, eds., *Zhuanyehu jingying guanli shouce*, p. 298.

13. Guojia gongshang xingzheng guanli ju geti jingji si, eds., *Geti gongshangye jiben qingquang tongji ziliao xuanbian 1949–1986.*

14. For example, Tang Congyao and Xu Youyi, eds., *Zhuanyehu getihu falü zixun shouce*, and Ma Zheng, Zhou Wei, and Song Heping, eds.,

Zhuanyehu getihu zhengce falü guwen, are full of examples in which administrative practice treats the two equally, according to their activities rather than their type.

15. The phrase "initial stage of socialism" (*shehuizhuyi de chuji jieduan*) was used early on in the individual economy debate, for example at an April 1981 conference on ownership held by the Chinese Academy of Social Sciences in Chengdu. See *Jingji wenti tansuo*, eds., *Zhongguo xian jieduan geti jingji yanjiu*.

16. He Jianzhang and Zhang Wenmin, "The System of Ownership: A Tendency Toward Multiplicity," p. 201. The same point is made by Fang Sheng, "The Revival of the Individual Economy in Certain Areas," p. 175.

17. *RMRB*, 20 June 1980, p. 5, quoted in Solinger, *Chinese Business*, p. 201.

18. He Jianzhang, "Jiji fuchi, shidang fazhan chengzhen geti jingji," p. 14.

19. On their role in earlier debates, see Cyril Chihren Lin, "The Reinstatement of Economics in China Today," pp. 26–34.

20. Dong Fureng, "Chinese Economy in the Process of Great Transformation," p. 128 (emphasis added). Dong also went further than most to address the implications for ownership of the attempt to introduce real market reforms, in a line of inquiry that was not actively pursued in public debate until 1985. See Dong Fureng, "Guanyu wo guo shehuizhuyi suoyouzhi xingshi wenti." See also the discussion in Cyril Zhiren Lin, "Open-Ended Economic Reform in China," p. 104.

21. See, for example, He Jianzhang, "Jiji fuchi," p. 14; *Jingji wenti tansuo*, eds., *Zhongguo xian jieduan*, p. 71. After the privatization debate was brought to a halt in June, 1989, an attempt was made to revive this line: see Chen Xin, "Lun siying jingji de fazhan jieduan."

22. Michel Bonnin and Michel Cartier, "Urban Employment in Post-Mao China."

23. Much of this paragraph is based on Carl Riskin, *China's Political Economy*, p. 267.

24. Fang, "Revival of Individual Economy," p. 180.

25. Chen Rengxing, "Shilun wo guo xian jieduan de geti jingji," p. 60.

26. Feng Lanrui and Zhao Lükuan, "Urban Unemployment in China," p. 136; Yuko Akiyoshi Nihei, "Unemployment in China: Policies, Problems and Proposals," p. 15.

27. For some figures on the post-1978 shift to light industry and consumption, see Stephen Feuchtwang and Athar Hussain, eds., *The Chinese Economic Reforms*, pp. 27–28.

28. More recently, the development of private businesses gave rise to spontaneous "cooperatives" of individual investors, but these evolved more in the direction of capitalist shareholding as private employers combined their resources in order to expand. See Wang Taixi, "Xi'an shi geti jingji de lishi he xianzhuang"; He Jianzhang and Zhu Qingfang, "Geti jingji de fazhan qishi ji duice"; also *RMRB*, 10 September 1985, p. 2; 1 March 1986, p. 2; 19 August 1986, p. 1; and 16 June 1988, p. 1.

29. Interview, Linfeng township, Anyue county, Sichuan, 26 February 1992.

30. Chinese Communist Party, "Resolution on Certain Questions in the History of Our Party," p. 78.

31. See, for example, the arguments in Xue Mou, "Zenyang zhengque renshi shehuizhuyi gaizao jiben wancheng yihou de xiao shengchan?" p. 42; Liu Long, ed., *Zhongguo xian jieduan geti jingji yanjiu*, p. 2; *Jingji wenti tansuo*, eds., *Zhongguo xian jieduan*, p. 6; Dong Fureng, "Chinese Economy," p. 128; and Chen Rengxing, "Xian jieduan de geti jingji," p. 61.

32. Qian Fenyong, "Fangshou fazhan chengzhen jiti geti jingji," p. 3.

33. He Jianzhang, "Jiji fuchi," p. 15.

34. Liu Long, ed., *Geti jingji yanjiu*, p. 5; Sun Ping, "Individual Economy under Socialism," p. 18.

35. See Yudkin, *Making Good*, p. 89.

36. See, for example, *RMRB*, 12 April 1988, p. 2; Liu Guoguang, "Socialism Is Not Egalitarianism"; Lin Zili, "Wenzhou shangpin jingji de 'chengfen' wenti."

37. Chen Rengxing, "Xian jieduan de geti jingji," p. 61; see also *Ha'erbin ribao* (Harbin Daily), 15 April 1983, p. 3; Liu Long, ed., *Geti jingji yanjiu*, p. 65. Here the insistence that China only allowed the small-scale "individual economy" stood reformist economists in good stead.

38. Xue Mou, "Zenyang zhengque renshi," pp. 42–43; see also *Beijing Review*, no. 33 (18 August 1980), p. 4; *Jingji wenti tansuo*, eds., *Zhongguo xian jieduan*, p. 53; Chen Rengxing, "Xian jieduan de geti jingji," p. 61. This argument, like the one about size, was progressively weakened by the very success of the reforms in increasing the role of free markets in commodities and finance.

39. Examples of this argument include He Jianzhang, "Jiji fuchi"; Chen Rengxing, "Xian jieduan de geti jingji"; and Liu Long, ed., *Geti jingji yanjiu*, p. 2.

40. Dong Fureng, "Chinese Economy," p. 128.

41. For example, Qian Fenyong, "Fangshou fazhan," p. 3.

3

Responses to the Private Sector Revival

Although the individual economy developed rapidly after 1978, its path was by no means free of obstacles. Opposition to the policy of promoting private business, only indirectly reflected in the debates surrounding it, was felt more overtly in the course of its actual implementation. Among consumers, attitudes about private business were ambivalent. Private businesspeople made life much more convenient, but they were also seen as low class, untrustworthy, and the possessors of an excessive and undeserved amount of wealth. Of key importance were the attitudes of those with power and influence over private businesspeople: the cadres in administrative departments and staff in state units with which private businesses had dealings. In the early stages of the reforms there was some direct opposition to private business among cadres, and this persisted to some extent, but the growth of the private sector also offered new opportunities to both individual cadres and their departments or localities. This meant that in addition to obstruction there was a parallel trend of exploiting or co-opting the private sector, which placed new con-

The first section of this chapter is based on Susan Young, "Wealth But Not Security: Attitudes towards Private Business in the 1980s," in *Economic Reform and Social Change in China*, ed. Andrew Watson (London and New York: Routledge, 1992). Reprinted with permission from the publishers.

straints on the way private business developed, but at least allowed it to do so.

Negative Perceptions of Private Business

Despite the general trend of official support from the central government, private entrepreneurs, particularly those in urban areas, had to contend with considerable opposition and social prejudice. This was particularly noticeable in the early years after 1978, when the private sector had yet to become well established. The political campaigns of the preceding thirty years, especially the Cultural Revolution, had inculcated the general concept that private enterprise was a bad thing, and that the bigger and "more public" an enterprise was, the better and more socialist. A 1983 *Renmin ribao* (People's Daily) article described the attitude toward individual business as "If individual business isn't capitalism, it's a tail of capitalism. Anyway it's not socialism."[1] A much-publicized letter to *Beijing ribao* (Beijing Daily) in August 1980 expressed horror at the revival of small private businesses, arguing (prophetically, as it turned out) that:

> A small-time premise today may well expand into a big one tomorrow. While capitalists of the old days are still living, new ones will before long come on the scene, with so many people intent on money-grubbing and so many small shops and roadside stalls cluttering the streets.[2]

This kind of prejudice appears to have been more typical of urban areas than of the countryside, where the impact of rural reforms meant that private enterprise became more integrated into the economy than in the cities. In urban areas, the majority of acknowledged private businesses were *getihu* engaged in pure commerce, seen as nonproductive and of dubious ethical standing, or in service trades such as catering or repairs—menial tasks for which many people maintained a strong disdain. Most *getihu* were involved in businesses of this type because they were easy and cheap to set up, often required no special knowledge or skill, and were in high demand.

It was these businesses, of course, that were the most visible and that interacted directly with the public, mostly by taking their money. Not surprisingly, their high incomes then engendered some resentment. This was exacerbated by the common and not entirely unfounded perception that most private operators cheated customers, charged overly high prices, obtained goods through illegal channels, and in general devoted themselves to taking as much as they could from society without contributing to it.

The low regard in which the private sector, and the fields in which it was concentrated, were held, compared to the state and collective sectors in urban areas, is seen most clearly in the marked resistance among urban youth to entering private employment. The ICB argued in the mid-1980s that this resistance had declined: the proportion of young people in private businesses registered as *getihu* increased from less than 10 percent initially to over 25 percent after 1985.[3] This was held to be a sign of improvement in the status of private business among urban youth, but it may have been the result largely of the influx of rural youth into cities and towns. Two sisters who started a hairdresser's in 1980 said, "We were worried because we did not feel that it was proper for young people to be self-employed,"[4] and a young man doing business in 1983 told how

> When I applied to do individual business, my friends and classmates were amazed. They said doing individual business had no political future, no security of livelihood, no social position, and even finding a girlfriend would be difficult.[5]

In fact this reluctance to enter private employment stemmed both from its lack of prestige and from practical considerations: state employment has been seen until very recently as an "iron rice bowl" offering lifetime security, while both state and collective employment were seen as far more secure politically. *Renmin ribao* commented in 1986 that

> For a long time, some people have had fixed in their minds the idea that "state is first, collective second, and individual is looked down

on"; they all want an "iron rice bowl." This has led to a contradiction as, on one hand, there are many people with nothing to do and, on the other, many things with no one doing them.[6]

Not least among the drawbacks of private business was that the private operator had to forgo the benefits obtained through a state or collective unit. Depending on the size and wealth of the unit, these included housing, access to childcare, education, health care, and retirement pensions, as well as the occasional load of cheap oranges or a free movie on National Day. And in a society constructed on the premise that all individuals would eventually be part of some collective organization, alternative channels for the provision of such benefits could be difficult to find even if one was willing to pay. When possible, people who wished to go into business kept a foot in both camps by maintaining links with a state unit. Many of the private entrepreneurs I interviewed in 1988 obtained housing and some other benefits through spouses or parents with state unit jobs. Without such arrangements private business looked less attractive, and some young school-leavers preferred to remain unemployed rather than take up private business, fearing that to do so would influence their chances of a "proper job" with a state or collective unit. To get around this problem labor bureaus generally continued to count them as *daiye qingnian* (youth awaiting employment) even after they were running a viable, full-time private business: "Their income is generally enough to keep two or three people, and yet they are still seen as 'job-waiting personnel' (*daiye renyuan*) and also see themselves in this way."[7] Economic problems in the late 1980s meant that the publicly owned sector continued to be incapable of providing jobs for all school-leavers, but many still remained unemployed for years at a stretch, with no hope of obtaining a state job, rather than go into business.[8]

Probably the major factor in the unwillingness of urban youth to engage in private business was its political insecurity. As well as economic risks, which may be exacerbated by discrimination or opposition, the private entrepreneur takes a political risk. The rise of the private sector is entirely the result of the reforms instituted since 1978, and past sudden changes in policy have not been forgotten. The passing of time and the continued growth of private business allayed fears of a change to some extent, but caution remained. When I asked a young woman in Chengdu in 1988 whether she would consider leaving her collective job to make three times as much money with her businesswoman sister, she said she wouldn't, because "You can't rely on state policy."[9] The conservative swing that accompanied the repression of the protest movement in 1989 no doubt confirmed her in this opinion.

Private business, therefore, appealed primarily to people who had little to lose by it—at least in the early years of the reforms. Many people starting private businesses in the late seventies and early eighties were the older unemployed, the miscellaneous "idle personnel" of the statistics who had been unable to find a permanent niche in the collective system.[10] An estimated 10 percent of individual businesses were run by ex-convicts who found it almost impossible to get a job in a state or collective unit.[11] In addition to people who had almost no hope of a "better" job, private business appealed to retired people who found their pensions inadequate. People who had left a state job to go into business for themselves or to be employed by a *siying qiye* nearly always sought to keep their options open by paying the unit to maintain benefits and to keep the job open (*ting xin liu zhi*) in case policies changed. In Chengdu in 1988, the going rate seemed to be around 50 percent of the person's former salary.

The fact that so many of the ordinary *getihu* were of low-status backgrounds tended to reinforce adverse perceptions of all private entrepreneurs, especially the unspectacular *getihu*: the view was that if they were decent people and had any standards, they would be doing something else. Schoolteachers claimed that the children of individual businesspeople were less intelligent and more disobedient than other children and remarked that this was because their parents were too busy making money to look after them properly.[12] A newspaper article reporting a rise in crimes committed by the offspring of *getihu* attributed this partly to the example set by their parents' "bad background" and illicit business activities.[13] Such assumptions may have been true in some cases; but whether true or not, discussions such as these both illustrate and reinforce negative attitudes toward private businesspeople.[14] The idea that private business was inferior persisted in spite of the rapid development of the private sector: for example, in 1988 a young woman I know in Chengdu would not sell eggs in the thriving market at the college near her home, but went elsewhere because her boyfriend lived at the college. "I couldn't! Imagine what people would say . . . Xiao Liu's girlfriend selling eggs!" At the time, she was spending some of the proceeds of her egg sales on "presents" so that she could get a job in a collective factory.

In rural areas, the situation was different. Although the countryside was as sensitive to political insecurity as the cities, the opportunity cost of going into private business was much lower. Rural residents, too, were people who had little to lose by going into business. They were not giving up the chance of security and welfare benefits by doing so: on the contrary, the income so gained would enhance their future security, and if private business were to be repressed again they would at worst be in the same position as before, only richer. They might even be better off in other ways too: private enterprise in rural areas was not associated with low status. It was in rural towns that the majority of the larger private enterprises, the *siying qiye*, developed, and as will be discussed in chapter 5, in terms of activities, management, wealth, and impact on the local economy these were quite a different matter from the urban image of a *getihu*. Rural private enterprise, particularly the larger concerns, became closely integrated with the rural elite.[15] Reports of local cadres pressuring private entrepreneurs to give jobs to their relatives indicate that in the rural setting, private employment could be seen as not only acceptable but even desirable.[16] In some areas the development of private enterprise led to a drain of skilled labor away from collective enterprises as people left to start up on their own or work for a private employer.[17] Private enterprise could also be a way of improving one's political position: the owners of larger, very successful private enterprises that were changed to collective status could then become government cadres, or in some cases private entrepreneurs were being voted into local government, because they were seen as having the right skills to lead the community in their footsteps to greater wealth.[18]

This difference between urban and rural perceptions of private business sheds light on the real barriers to its development and how they were overcome. The official approach to the problem of cadres blocking or harassing private business generally put it down to prejudice and disagreement with reform policies, but the fact that both rural and urban businesses were plagued by similar problems suggests that there were also other reasons. Attacks on the private sector were in fact often motivated not by antagonism to the reforms, but by competition for the benefits of those reforms between the collective and private sectors, with cadres using all the nonmarket, bureaucratic powers given to them in the pre-reform era to fight in the marketplace.

Barriers to Private Business

In the early 1980s there were constant complaints that cadres were discriminating against private businesses and seeking to hinder their growth. There were many reasons for this, which will be discussed in greater detail below. One set of reasons stemmed from the general attitudes toward private business described above: political antipathy to private enterprise could lead to direct attacks on it, or the less antagonistic position of simply looking down on private operators could lead administrators to ignore their interests. But there were also other reasons. Some "discrimination" appears to have resulted merely from bureaucratism and the relatively powerless position of the private entrepreneur. The usually small-scale, always independent private businesses were often inconvenient for the established system to deal with, and bureaucrats, accustomed to working within a top-down, state-controlled system, were sometimes slow to adapt to the diversity of new conditions. In the early years they were often not sure that it was wise to do so: if policies changed again, would they be criticized for encouraging capitalism? This mistrust of policy was reflected in periodic downturns in private sector growth, which can be linked directly to fluctuations in policy at the central level.

Private businesses are licensed and administered by the ICB, a national organization under the State Council, or in some rural areas they are administered by the Township Enterprise Bureaus (*xiangzhen qiye ju*) under the Ministry of Agriculture. Naturally, they also come into contact with various other bureaucracies in charge of local government, taxation, health, public order, town planning, marketing, and so on. As the reforms took shape through the 1980s these organizations jostled for position in the changing reform environment. The relationships between them were complex, and their respective responsibilities were often unclear or overlapping. This situation provided a fertile environment for personal or departmental empire-building by cadres and gave them wide scope to act according to interests that might not coincide with central policies. Cadre attitudes toward private business were neither unified nor unchanging, but reflected their perception of their interests at any given time. Private businesses both suffered and benefited from this situation. The reform process set up built-in incentives that encouraged local-level officials to promote private business, and as a reform-oriented culture developed, obstruction of private business tended to give way to qualified support.

The Political Insecurity of Private Business

Direct opposition to private business was most clearly expressed in harassment of private operators, including forcing private operators to move to less favorable sites, unauthorized confiscation of licenses, closing businesses for investigation, levying excessive and punitive fines and charges, and ransacking of premises and confiscation of goods. Isolated cases of such harassment can be found at any time, but during the 1980s there were also several concentrated waves of anti-private activity, stimulated by changes in the central balance of power between the more radical reformers and those who were more concerned about stability and order. Central calls to slow down the reforms, cool down the economy, or "rectify the market" were reflected in a reduced rate of growth in the private economy.

The variability in central politics naturally made it difficult for local cadres to know how to approach the politically sensitive private sector. As an editorial in the reformist paper *Shichang* (The Market) put it in 1981,

> Some leading departments treat the individual economy, not according to policy, but according to the way the wind blows. They think the policy of allowing the individual economy is merely an expedient measure, so when there is an opportunity, they change tack.[19]

The first of these changes in the wind occurred in late 1980. State cadres argued that the market was becoming chaotic because of too much freedom and, on the pretext of "rectifying the market" and "attacking speculation," began to crack down on private traders. Not only commercial departments, but departments of health, city appearance, urban construction, public security, and taxation all began to impinge upon private traders, and often confiscated licenses.[20] In some places the number of registered individual businesses dropped by as much as 50 percent in the first half of 1981.[21] This was apparently a reflection of the debate in progress at the central level over the extent of marketization and decentralization; there was a feeling among the more conservative leaders, such as Chen Yun, that reforms were running out of control and that the reduction in central control was leading to overinvestment in capital construction and consequently exacerbating sectoral imbalances and inflationary pressures.[22]

In 1983, the drive against spiritual pollution was also reflected in attacks on private business. While the trend of central policy was toward further liberalization, the government was anxious that this should not lead to economic and social disorder. Therefore while some restrictions were removed, efforts were made to clamp down on cheating, high prices, tax evasion, and the like. In 1983 a series of central and local regulations on the licensing and control of individual businesses, taxation, product quality and hygiene, and free markets were introduced and were followed by inspection drives. Here again, cadres acted "not according to policy but according to how the wind blows," and market rectification drives became an opportunity to attack private business, as when Wuhan police closed down over five hundred private stalls, accusing them of causing environmental and traffic problems.[23] Marcia Yudkin's book on the individual economy tells how, in Shandong, the growth of the private sector caused some cadres and state enterprises to argue that it had developed too much, and some of the more Left-leaning cadres started to revoke licenses.[24] Beijing's cleanup drive reportedly caused more than seven thousand *getihu* to close down.[25] This interpretation of the drive to improve control of commercial activity probably reflected the political atmosphere of the time: the effort to slow down economic growth and the campaign against spiritual pollution were interpreted by some as a setback, and potential reversal, in the process of reform.[26]

One issue clearly related to the anti–spiritual pollution campaign was that of *getihu* running businesses associated with leisure and entertainment. Here the "Dao Shizhuang" teahouse was something of a test case, reported in the national press in May 1984.[27] According to the reports, Su Daoshan, a young unemployed man in Beijing, applied to run a teahouse in May 1983, but was told that he could deal only in cakes, wine, cigarettes, and so on, not tea. Su then appealed to the Beijing ICB, which approved the teahouse. In October, however, the mayor of Beijing announced a rectification drive (part of the national drive described above) aimed at the city's *getihu*, and the district ICB closed down the teahouse on the grounds that tea and cakes were two separate lines of business (not then allowed), and that tea-houses were socially unnecessary. Citing Lao She's *Teahouse* as evidence, they added that the teahouse attracted undesirable customers and was the thin end of the wedge in the line from teahouse to bar to "nightclub." Eventually, however, the reformists' refusal to allow the anti–spiritual pollution campaign to impinge upon economic growth was reflected in the teahouse question. Su Daoshan's teahouse reopened, and in August 1984 no less than three central ministries—Commerce, Environmental Protection and Urban and Rural Construction, and Labor—combined with the ICB to publish a notice on actively encouraging and even organizing *getihu* to run teahouses.[28]

Sometimes incidents reported in the press as harassment of private business could also be interpreted as officials merely following the letter of the law and illustrate the difficulties faced by officials in administering private business under changing conditions. *Renmin ribao* in January 1983 criticized civilian defense personnel and sanitation inspectors in a case involving a retired woman and her daughter who were selling fruit and tobacco from a cart. The officials said that the cart was an eyesore, was in a street barred to private traders, and that the girl's license was for her alone, not her mother. The two refused to hand over the cart and were "beaten up" by the officials.[29] While beating up the women sounds excessive, the officials may well have been right about the pair's violation of regulations. In another case, a private tailor was able to buy cloth without coupons from her husband, a deputy director of a supply and marketing co-op branch. When this illegal arrangement was discovered, the relevant departments investigated and took the case to court. The husband was jailed for one year, and their profits, meticulously detailed in the newspaper as consisting of 1,855 yuan, a twelve-inch black-and-white television, a wristwatch, and seventy-seven unsold pieces of clothing, were confiscated.[30] The interesting thing about this case is that it was reported, not as an example of a back-door dealer coming to a sticky end, but as a case of "red-eye disease," or jealousy, on the part of the prosecuting officials.

Both stories illustrate that officials *do* have to act "not according to policy, but according to the way the wind blows." In the rapidly changing conditions of reform, regulations were quickly out of date, and central policy documents were vague and open to interpretation. Bureaucrats were expected to apply regulations with a certain amount of discretion, and it was their interpretation of the political climate that prompted them to lean to Left or Right, to encourage private business or restrict it.

The rate of growth of the private economy was a reflection not solely of political fluctuations but also of economic conditions, the more so as the private sector grew and became more integrated with other ownership sectors. This appears to have been the case with the downturn in private sector growth rates, reported in the first half of 1986. At this time, the amount of credit available to both *getihu* and state and collective enterprises had been curtailed, and there were renewed efforts to improve tax collection and market administration. Again, the economic conditions also had a political dimension, since any such tightening of economic policies was interpreted by some administrators, and by many private entrepreneurs, as a sign of a more general leftward policy shift. Furthermore, in the economic downturn officials tended to support state and collective enterprises and see the private economy as a threat to them.[31] In that period, according to one source, the number of registered individual businesses fell by 2.6 percent nationally, by 9.4 percent in Liaoning, and by 9.3 percent in its capital, Shenyang.[32] Similar falls in numbers of both *getihu* and *siying qiye* were reported in various other locations, including Shanghai, Shanxi, Jiangxi, and Inner Mongolia.[33] State Statistical Bureau figures do not show a drop in registered *getihu* numbers, but they do show a huge decline in the number of people entering private employment in urban areas, from 1.1 million in 1985 to 330,000 in 1986.[34] This time, the decline in the private sector was blamed partly on attacks by cadres, but more often on excessive fees and fines. There was also a new element in the explanations, as some newspaper reports, as well as ICB cadres I interviewed in Zigong in 1988, sought to give the impression that there had in fact been no real decline in growth rates, or if there was, it had been the result of market forces in action: after the rapid growth of 1984–85, there were too many *getihu* in certain trades, and some had naturally gone out of business.[35] However, administrators tended to decide for themselves that too many *getihu* were in a particular trade or area and refuse to grant any more licenses except for businesses they saw as beneficial.[36]

The major setback in private sector growth that occurred in 1989 was also the result of a combination of political and economic (albeit partly politically induced) factors. The attack on private business actually began well before June 1989, as concern mounted about economic disorder, confused administration, inflation, and corruption. Private businesses first suffered from the drive to improve control over market activity and clean up business administration launched in the autumn of 1988. In late 1988 the ICB began to pressure private businesses that had managed to register as collectives (of which there were many) to register as private, and in the first half of 1989 it conducted a nationwide drive to inspect and relicense all private businesses.[37] In the tense political climate of the time, these moves were seen by some private business operators as a sign of imminent policy changes, and by some cadres as a signal to go hard on the private sector.[38] The June crackdown, of course, confirmed this trend, and private businesses were made a clear target for attack. They were accused of large-scale tax evasion and blamed for much of the corruption in the economy and for high prices as well.[39] The new austerity program affected private entrepreneurs, who could no longer get loans, found it harder to find customers, and in some cases were not even allowed to withdraw their money from banks.[40] As a result of these combined factors, the private sector showed significant falls in 1989, with the number of registered private businesses dropping by over 14 percent.[41] As Table 1.1 (page 6) shows, license numbers did not recover their 1988 levels until 1992, when private sector growth increased rapidly after Deng Xiaoping's Southern Tour speeches again gave the green light to growth-focused policies.

Limiting Private Competition

Apart from direct attacks, the impact of cadres' interpretation of the political climate can be seen in many reports of cadres placing excessive limits on private businesses. Cadres often took advantage of local discretionary powers to block the growth of the individual economy wherever possible. In the early years of reform the central policy of "appropriate development" of the individual economy was sometimes interpreted to mean very little development indeed: one county in Hebei considered that an appropriate number of individual businesses, for its more than 400,000 residents, was just seven, although 100 more had also applied.[42] A common way of blocking individual businesses was to make them seek approval from numerous different departments before a license could be granted, thus greatly increasing the opportunities for bureaucratic delay. The 1981 regulations on the individual economy stated that individuals must have the approval of their local street committee and obtain the license from their local ICB branch, although those engaging in businesses relating to education, culture, and health were subject to separate regulation by the relevant departments. In rural areas, individuals required the approval of local governments at both township and county level before obtaining a license from the ICB.[43] Yet in practice agreements were made between the various departments so that the ICB issued a license only after approval was given by departments responsible for city planning, hygiene, public security, energy or raw material supplies if applicable, public security, and so on. Not only was approval from various departments required, but this in turn had to pass through various levels of these organizations. The owner of a private take-out stall in Nanjing, for example, had to make more than twenty trips to gain permission to switch to photo-processing.[44] These requirements differed from place to place, trade to trade, and time to time, the trend being to simplify procedures in later years.

In some places limits were imposed not so much on the number of private businesses as on their activities. In Tianjin there was at first a regulation that individuals using bicycle carts had to stay within one district or be fined—most inconvenient for private transporters.[45] (Admittedly, it is difficult to determine whether this rule was designed to limit private businesses or to make money from them.) A letter to *Renmin ribao* in 1986 complained that although private barbers were a great convenience to the public, the one the writer patronized was hard to find because it was tucked away in a lane and not allowed to put a sign on the street.[46] Private businesspeople often claimed that they were discriminated against in this way; that they were accused of obstructing traffic, disturbing the peace, or ruining the city's appearance, when similar shops run by state or collective units were not.

One reason for discrimination against private entrepreneurs was that they were seen as competitors with the (ideologically and morally superior) public sector and thus, by extension, as potential saboteurs of socialism. This led to obstruction and discrimination against private business, not only by enterprises that felt directly threatened, but by a wide range of administrators and staff members who saw their interests as being aligned with the state-run system. The community of interests between state enterprises and state administrative departments led them to form a coalition against private business, acting defensively against an erosion of their security:

> The system of government and enterprises being united makes some people in charge of economic matters consider and deal with problems from the point of view of state shops, and see individual businesses as a fearsome competitive force against state commerce, so they consciously or unconsciously squeeze it out.[47]

As noted above, many early arguments in favor of the individual economy emphasized its subordinate, supplementary nature and suggested that individual businesses would generally engage in trades in which the state sector had no interest. However there was another, important stream in the pro-individual economy case that argued competition from an independent private sector was necessary to stimulate sluggish state enterprises to better service and greater efficiency. State enterprises were notorious for their lack of responsiveness to customer demands, particularly in the area of consumer goods and services, at which the promotion of private business was particularly aimed. Given a lack of alternatives, it was difficult for consumers to communicate their demands effectively to state enterprises in the first place. The reformist goal of increased efficiency required incentives, and incentives could be effective only in conditions in which consumers could choose between good products or service and bad, so that an enterprise's performance could have immediate and measurable consequences. Some critics of Soviet-style socialism have suggested that this element of choice, an independent alternative to the state system, is necessary as a measure and a stimulant of state sector performance.[48]

In the Chinese context, several factors—in particular the relative size of the private sector in terms of output value or turnover, the immense demand for the products and services in which it specialized, the continued soft budget constraint in state enterprises, and the preferential treatment given to state and collective enterprises—lessened the impact of private competition on the public sector, although these factors were weakened as the reform process continued. It is nevertheless clear that both state and collective enterprises were aware of private businesses as a threat. There was both a political and an economic dimension to their perceptions of the issue. Many cases have been reported of responses by state and collective enterprises that saw private businesses as an economic threat. Their tactics ranged from direct physical assault, to lobbying local officials, to—apparently as a last resort—reforming their own practices in order to cope with the competition economically.

On an enterprise-to-enterprise level, private businesses proved capable of providing public enterprises with real competition. To counter the state units' advantages of size and connections, private businesses generally had lower overheads and, because their operators were directly dependent on the businesses for their income, strong incentives to operate efficiently. This argument was often repeated in Chinese discussions of private business: one Chinese study gives the example of a Shanghai manufacturer of brassieres and collars. Using offcuts bought cheaply from a shirt factory, the operator made brassieres at a total cost of 31 fen each, and sold them wholesale for 40 fen. The authors compare this with a state factory that, using good bolt cloth, made them at a cost per item of 58 fen.[49] Like most such comparisons it is extremely unfair, since it implies that the state unit's high costs stem purely from inefficiencies and ignores the burden of its employee welfare provisions.

In some cases, staff of state enterprises threatened by private businesses responded by attacking and harassing the offending business. The staff of rival restaurants seem to have been particularly prone to smashing up each other's food bowls: in 1980 "angry personnel of a state-operated restaurant vented their wrath by smashing the dishes of nearby food stalls,"[50] and in 1984 one Wu Taoying had a similar problem. Having been rash enough to set up a take-out food stall next door to a state-run restaurant, she proceeded to outshine the restaurant with her low prices and cheerful service. Rather than improving their own standards, restaurant staff overturned her stall and forced her out of business.[51]

The alliance between state and collective enterprises and administrative cadres is illustrated by press reports detailing cases in which enterprises of these types used their superior political and economic connections to respond to private competition. In July 1984, for example, *Renmin ribao* published an account of the tribulations of Qin Yujie, a peasant in Liaoning who, "in order to solve the local transport problem," started a private bus service. His state-run competitor used its influence to persuade bus station officials to impound his bus. When this action was overturned by higher authorities, the state company added four more buses to the route in question. These buses not only took most of the customers, but attempted to run the private bus off the road. Since the state company could afford to run the route at a loss and repair damaged buses much better than the private operator could, it was a very unequal battle.[52] In another case, a county supply and marketing cooperative blamed its falling turnover on private business, and persuaded local authorities to revoke nine hundred licenses at one sweep. (The newspaper article criticizing this action smugly reported that the cooperative's turnover failed to improve.)[53] The competition between private and collective enterprises in rural areas was in fact much more direct than between the urban public and private sectors, and rural local governments acted to defend collective interests in a variety of ways, for example, by appropriating successful private enterprises or by forcing them out of business and replacing them with a collective enterprise of the same kind.[54]

The reformist response to such problems was a campaign to criticize enterprises and cadres who attempted to block private enterprise and to point out the advantages of "healthy competition." Some press reports did this by detailing cases of successful cooperation between state and private enterprise, such as the Hunan Motor Transport Corporation, which initially feared competition from private transporters and sought to hinder them. In August 1984, however, the company saw the error of its ways, and began to see private transporters as an opportunity instead, using its superior resources to offer them services such as loading stations, mechanical repairs, and training, with the result that its own profits rose rather than fell.[55] A similar response, of moving into a different market, was reported in Shenyang. State restaurants, greatly outnumbered by collective and private operations, used their better facilities and connections to specialize in the up-market banquet trade, leaving everyday off-the-street customers to their competitors. A similar phenomenon occurred in photo-processing: when color photos first came onto the scene, the state shops were able to import the equipment, while the black-and-white trade was left to private operators.[56] This advantage could only have been short term, however, as private color photo-processing shops soon appeared in Chinese streets, often cooperating with a state unit that did the actual processing. However, as the case of the bus company cited above illustrates, the advantages of state-run enterprises with respect to funds, premises, and connections are considerable, should they elect to use them. As one private businessperson pointed out, if the state enterprises want to compete, they have many advantages. "To tell the truth, the state shops' wealth and influence, their wide connections, are something we individuals have no way of competing with."[57] This sentiment was echoed by the manager of a non-state bank in Chengdu, whose clientele included some of Chengdu's largest and most successful private enterprises, when I interviewed him in 1988. "The success of the private economy is based on the shortcomings of state enterprises. If the state enterprises really start to compete, private enterprise had better watch out." The state enterprises' dislike of competition stemmed not from their fear of losing the fight, but from the fact that winning it required hard work, longer hours, better service, and changes in organization that were often difficult to make at the enterprise level. These changes did begin to occur as reforms to make state enterprises more profit-oriented began to take effect after 1984, but the whole point of the "iron rice bowl" is that it is hard to crack.

A parallel stream of behavior, which gained strength as the reforms continued, was seeing private businesses as an easy target for graft and blackmail, and there were constant complaints that private businesses were seen as "fat meat to be arbitrarily cut up." Departments, or their staff acting as individuals, had many opportunities to impose charges or fines at will. Private businesses, being very dependent on the personal goodwill of people in charge of the goods, energy and raw materials, and administrative approvals they needed, were very easy targets for personal extortion by these people. Individual staff members of administrative or supply departments often used this situation to extort "gifts" or free services from private businesses before a permit was issued or fuel, water, electricity, or raw materials supplied.

A typical illustration of this is the story of Chu Ruitang, as told in *Renmin ribao* in 1987. Chu leased a restaurant in 1986 and, in order to open for business, needed a hygiene inspection certificate and a business license. Chu was repeatedly told that the relevant departments were "too busy" to inspect the restaurant, although they did not look very busy to him. Only after a friend explained that "presents" were necessary to get things done did Chu make any progress. He got his hygiene certificate for a case of wine, and his license for the cost of a banquet. But after opening, his problems continued, as price inspectors, the local coal supply station, the police, the local bank branch director, and the water company all required him to supply them with free meals (the coal station demanded dumplings for forty people at short notice), wine, and cigarettes.[58] The newspaper's commentary on the case observed:

> Some people just need to get a little bit of power and be in charge of something, for example water, electricity, coal, household registration, loans, licensing, hygiene certificates, and so on, and then they use every opportunity to wantonly use this power to their own advantage, and furthermore feel justified in doing so. This has become a public menace.[59]

Restaurants appear to have been particularly popular targets for this sort of extortion—perhaps because an official with whom the restaurateur needed to be on good terms could then wine and dine other officials with whom he or she needed to be on good terms, and all for free. This could sometimes make heavy demands on a business: for example, one individual who invested 1,800 yuan to start up his business had, over a period of about eight months, supplied free services to the value of 1,300 yuan.[60] In the much-publicized case of Tianmen county, Hubei, cadres had extracted a total of 42,000 yuan from individual businesses and specialized households.[61]

More important than individual extortion were levies by various local administrative and supply departments and local governments. Private businesses could be charged fees for road occupation, city appearance, traffic regulation, sanitation, and numerous other items. Sometimes they even had to pay the same type of fee to more than one department, for example a "road occupation fee" to both the city planning office and the department of public roads.[62] In Chengdu in 1988, individual businesses could end up paying as many as twenty-nine different fees of this kind, some on a regular basis and some imposed only occasionally as part of government "drives" for children's health, road construction, town beautification, and the like.[63] In one Sichuan example, a private enterprise that paid 10,000 yuan in taxes had paid 7,600 yuan for just two local fees in the same year.[64] A 1992 report from Henan stated that in some areas irregular charges on *siying qiye* added up to over twice the amount of regulated taxes.[65]

The real importance of these levies is that they are a source of local revenue almost immune to central control. They often are not reported to higher levels, but are hidden income. For local governments this is useful because it will not lead to a higher revenue quota and goes straight to local uses. A 1988 study of villages and townships in Renshou county, Sichuan, found that the income they obtained from private businesses was at least as much again as payments of centrally regulated taxes and that a large part of this was never reported to county level.[66] Private businesspeople complain of these charges because they are irregular, unpredictable, and often exorbitant. The central government complains about them for these reasons too, but also because they are an uncontrolled source of local revenue that takes money away from the centrally regulated tax system.

Ironically, these burdensome levies have probably been a major factor in the growth of private business. They certainly have not been so heavy as to prevent it, and they have given local officials a direct incentive to support it.

Counteracting Negative Attitudes

During the 1980s, the media and certain government agencies conducted a series of campaigns to improve the image of private business. The aims were threefold: to encourage people to take up private business, to reassure those who had done so that they would not later be attacked, and to cultivate public acceptance of this aspect of reform policies. The media campaign began by tackling political opposition to private business, stressing the importance of private business to China's economic development, and associating its opponents with the unpopular Cultural Revolution by accusing them of incorrect "Left" ideas.

By the time private business had become extensive after 1983, a walk down almost any Chinese street was all that was needed to show how much private businesses had improved consumer services. The proliferation of private stalls and shops had brought goods closer to people's homes, provided a choice of outlets, and widened the range of goods and services available: many private operators revived traditional handicrafts and specialty foods that were disappearing under the previous system. The increased variety was also the result of the mobility of individual operators, who did well by taking their local speciality to another city where it was a novelty.

The benefits of promoting private business were highlighted by articles pointing out how much more convenient life was now that private shops were offering repairs, haircuts, fresh fruit, and innumerable small goods and services that were formerly provided inadequately or not at all by state enterprises. *Renmin ribao* and other newspapers published stories highlighting the contrast between surly or inconvenient state-run services and the private alternative. In one typical article, the author had taken a watch to several repair shops, all of which said it could not be repaired. Finally the author took the watch to a young private repairer, who not only repaired the watch, but later wrote asking if the repair had been satisfactory.[67] A private restaurateur in Sichuan was pictured with an award received for her services to consumers; the caption pointed out that she stuck to a policy of a small profit margin and high turnover, and made life much more convenient for peasants going into the city to sell produce.[68]

A great deal of emphasis was placed on the role of private businesses in simply providing *more* goods and services, as well as better service than state shops. Harbin's daily newspaper reported in 1983 that the threefold increase in retail and service outlets since 1978 was the result of the policy of "state, collective, and individual advancing together" (*guoying, jiti, geti yiqi shang*). Collective outlets had more than tripled in number, while individual outlets had increased more than tenfold, providing jobs for 71,000 youths awaiting job assignments.[69] In 1987, *Renmin ribao* noted that the same policy had improved rural health services. Since the state alone had been unable to provide adequate health care, especially in rural areas, various collective, individually contracted, or privately established medical services were a good way of making up the shortfall. According to the paper, the state had already approved over 133,000 private medical personnel who, because they had no "iron rice bowl," gave excellent service.[70] At other times a number of articles and readers' letters also appeared in the Chinese press casting doubts upon this last assertion, saying that private doctors often had little or no training,[71] but those campaigning in favor of private businesses tended to gloss over its less savory side and emphasized the connection between the operator's good reputation and his or her income.

The private economy was also advanced as a way of enlivening the economy in outlying, less developed areas, and of increasing exchange between country and city. By 1985, more than 2,000 individual traders from other provinces were operating in Tibet, bringing foods from Sichuan and Qinghai, daily necessities from Gansu, cloth and clothing from Guangzhou, electrical goods from Shanghai, and thus "enlivening the backward economy."[72] The Tibetan minority autonomous region of Yushu in Qinghai was reported to have benefited from opening its doors to individual traders from other provinces, most of whom were itinerant peddlers who traveled the grasslands to the great convenience of the isolated people there.[73] A 1989 article in *Jingji cankao* (Economic Information) again extolled the benefits that tailors from Zhejiang had brought to Lhasa: it was now possible for reporters from Beijing to have a pair of trousers made in a few hours.[74]

Another aspect of the campaign attempted to counteract the

poor image of private operators by reporting on "model" businesspeople who, having "gotten rich first," now paid their taxes, went out of their way to serve people well, made donations to charity, and were generally nice to have around. These articles were designed both to improve the image of private businesspeople and to give them models to emulate. The most serious attempt at a "model" campaign was that surrounding Xing Fuqiang, who was basically Lei Feng (the self- sacrificing model soldier first publicized in 1963) reincarnated as a private glazier, complete with an untimely death from cancer and a diary full of thoughts like "wholeheartedly serving the people is the greatest honor in my life."[75] In contrast to the popular image of the private operator who had eyes only for profits, Xing seriously wanted to make a contribution to society and would go to great lengths to help people, like walking many miles to repair a window for an old lady free of charge. Xing Fuqiang's case was unusual in that he was held up as a model not only for other private operators but for Youth League and party members to study as well.[76]

Outstanding private businesspeople were also honored at meetings. The most notable of these was in August 1983, when party General Secretary Hu Yaobang and other leaders received 609 advanced collective and individual representatives. Their speeches emphasized the role of collective and private business in providing jobs and reiterated that private employment was perfectly respectable.[77] A similar public relations exercise surrounded the establishment of the national-level Individual Laborers' Association in December 1986.[78] National newspapers ran numerous articles on the importance of private business and the propriety of private employment, including a front-page photograph in *Renmin ribao* of Zhao Ziyang, then premier, shaking hands with a private entrepreneur.[79]

Overcoming Constraints: The Impact of New Incentives

Much more significant than propaganda campaigns, the wider environment of economic reform generated a number of incentives for local officials to support the development of private business. Importantly, the way in which reforms were implemented allowed an increasing degree of leeway for local officials to adapt new policies and regulations to fit local conditions. In many cases this enabled the private sector to develop very rapidly, but it did so in an under-regulated, informal way, dominated by local interests and local administration.

The initial stimulus for the rapid development of private industry and commerce in rural China was the introduction of the household responsibility system, which led rural families to diversify their economic activities, market their surplus output, and invest in nonagricultural enterprises. In fact, the growth of private business was a vital corollary of the responsibility system, providing the markets, transport, inputs, consumer goods, and employment alternatives needed for it to succeed.

The household responsibility system created the environment for private business to develop, but the real boost to its growth came with the introduction of fiscal contracting between each level of government from province to county and down to township and village level. Introduced experimentally at provincial level from 1977, this had become widespread by 1985.[80] Local governments, having contracted to fulfill a revenue target, were made more responsible for their expenses as well as being allowed to retain a portion of their revenue and invest it as they saw fit. This gave them not only the incentive but also the wherewithal to develop new enterprises in their localities. Under this system, local governments also held considerable discretion in the actual calculation and sourcing of revenue collection and were able to manage their local economy, as Jean Oi and others have observed, like a corporation, using the profits from some enterprises to shore up others.[81] This gave them strong incentives to develop the private economy in excess of official policy and regulations, and use it as a little-regulated, extra-budgetary source of revenue.[82] Although it is impossible to quantify, at least some of the private sector's contribution in this respect is through the unauthorized local charges mentioned above.

While direct local government investment was naturally in collective enterprises and local infrastructure and services, the general incentives for economic development also promoted private enterprise in conditions where there were opportunities for small-scale, low- technology enterprises and where collectives did not have the funds to develop industry and commerce themselves. Under these conditions, some localities have developed successfully by relying on the "(Anhui) Fuyang model" of small-scale enterprise by many households, typically in conjunction with the development of specialized markets in one or more commodities. Although the evidence is far from complete, and local policies have varied widely, studies like that by Byrd and Lin and Ji and Zhu suggest that areas with a well-developed collective industry sector have tended to support it and either neglect private enterprise or restrict it for fear of competition. In contrast, poorer areas have often been only too happy to use all means available to improve their economic situation, although the Byrd and Lin studies suggest that in these areas, too, local governments will be more inclined to exploit enterprises for revenue.[83]

As a result of the incentives for promoting or at least allowing private business, many of the limits in central regulations were disregarded in practice. The State Council's 1981 regulations on the urban individual economy imposed strict limits on the scale and type of private businesses, but these were soon found to be impractical and either removed or ignored. The rules limiting individual businesses to nonmechanized tools and vehicles was impractical even for very small businesses. If private businesses were to help develop the commodity economy and supplement limited state investment capability, there was not much point in keeping them at an artificially backward level and encouraging operators to fritter their incomes away on consumption. If they were to "fill up the gaps" left by the state and collective sectors in, say, transport, they could hardly be expected to do so with shoulder-poles alone. Nor could such a restricted private sector realistically be expected to provide enough competition to help stimulate state and collective units to greater efficiency. Since the reformists measured their success by economic indicators, and the whole thrust of their program was to encourage decision-making based on economic factors, the private sector was allowed to grow in order to achieve economic goals.

For example, the regulations on the individual economy retained the limit on the number of people an individual could employ, and yet private businesses with over seven employees appeared as early as 1981, while officials "studied the question."[84] In this case, the goal of increasing employment was of paramount importance, but larger businesses also meant more investment, more spending, and a more vigorous local economy. Under a reformist government, this meant more credit to the leaders of that economy, as well as increased local revenue. Therefore individual businesses were given "temporary" permits to employ over seven people or were registered as collectives, or the problem was just ignored. This issue of the number of people an individual might employ was an important and contentious one in the development of private business, and it was not until 1988 that the party officially came to grips with it and the constitution was revised to include larger private enterprises among the types specifically allowed.

Very often as a recognition of established practice rather than as an innovation, many restrictive regulations came to be removed, at city and provincial level in 1982 and centrally in 1983. In 1982, for example, Shanghai issued a set of regulations on the individual economy that removed restrictions on the age of people who could undertake private business and the limit of one line of business per operator.[85] In November 1982, a national work conference on commerce loosened marketing restrictions on a variety of nonessential goods, and allowed traders as well as peasant producers to engage in long-distance wholesale and retail trade.[86] In June 1983 the State Council issued a set of supplementary regulations to the 1981 regulations on the urban individual economy that permitted individual businesses to use mechanized tools and vehicles, and to engage in long-distance and wholesale trade. The State Council's March 1983 guidelines on promoting the retail and service industries also sought to encourage private business in these activities by removing restrictions on sources of supply. Whereas individual businesses had previously been officially restricted to buying from approved state supply organs and in fact bought a portion of their supplies from other channels, they were now officially allowed to buy direct from factory surpluses and from other provinces.[87] The June supplementary regulations on the individual economy reiterated the widening of supply channels, although they also took care to emphasize that this applied only to goods outside or surplus to state plans. The danger, which proved to be very real, was that producers would prefer the higher prices paid by private businesses, and divert goods earmarked for the state plan to private buyers instead. This was a major factor in the nature and development of private business, which will be discussed further in chapter 4.

Whereas the stimulus of further liberalization of policy in 1983 was tempered by the strong emphasis on increasing market order and the political spin-off from the anti–spiritual pollution campaign, 1984 was a different matter. The campaign against spiritual pollution was discarded, and the central leadership was once again pushing for further reform. The Central Committee's Document No. 1 opened the year by taking rural reforms even further, urging increased commoditization of the rural economy.[88] It also acknowledged and approved rural private enterprises, including those in which individuals employed large numbers of people. This was followed in February by the State Council's Regulations on Rural Individual Industry and Commerce, the first national regulations acknowledging rural private business.[89] These regulations noted that the rural individual economy was important to "promoting the rural commodity economy, enlivening urban-rural circulation, and utilizing rural surplus labor" and are similar to the 1983 regulations on urban individual business although more specific concerning legitimate sources of supply.

Although Document No. 1 concerned itself solely with rural reform —improving the production responsibility system and encouraging peasants to invest in commodity production—it had a major impact on attitudes toward private business of all kinds, not only in the countryside and small towns, but in cities as well. For if peasants were to be encouraged to engage in more sideline commodity production and invest in industry, (i.e., in private businesses of their own), businesses such as the transport of passengers and goods, resale of rural produce, and buying urban consumer goods for resale in rural areas would all need to expand as well.

By 1984 the changes to the fiscal system and the removal of some restrictions were already providing impetus to private business development, but it is also clear that after the release of Document No. 1, city- and county-level administrative departments were directed to take concrete steps to promote the individual economy. In Linxi county, Hebei, for example, the ICB held meetings on how to improve services to individual businesses, and after April 1984 actually began to go out door to door to try and issue more licenses, whereas individuals had previously had to come to them. ICB personnel now took a photographer along with them and issued licenses on the spot, in marked contrast to the earlier laborious licensing process. As a result, by July the number of individual business licenses in the county had increased by 160 percent over 1983.[90] The newspapers of 1984 are scattered with reports of similar licensing drives throughout China, and these drives were usually accompanied by other measures to make it easier to do private business. The ICB in the city of Wuzhong in Ningxia, for example, removed the previous rule that a private operator could engage in only one line of business at a time, set up new marketplaces and stalls using ICB funds, built a hostel for peasants and transporters who came to do business, sent teams out to issue licenses in outlying towns, and used bulletin boards and broadcasts to provide market information to private traders.[91] In December 1984, the Liaoning provincial government issued a notice on protecting the legal rights of individual businesses, which included the stipulation that licensing procedures should be simplified and that the relevant departments should take no more than five days to process applications, or ten in the case of the city construction department.[92]

These all-out drives to promote private business were obviously a response to directives from above. Similar directives had been issued before and ignored, but in 1984 they were part of a much wider push for further market-oriented development. Many local cadres again saw the way the wind blew, and acted accordingly. ICB cadres were responsible for private business development in their region and often identified with private operators and championed their cause, while increased local control over revenue acted as an incentive for other cadres to support private business also. Although the growth rate of the individual economy was to drop again in response to the economic retrenchment of 1986, 1984 began a trend of much more comprehensive support of private business by the ICB. It not only simplified licensing procedures, but also became actively involved in solving other problems of private businesses. In 1988 cadres in Ling county, Shandong, had a quota of new individual business licenses to issue, with a bonus if they filled it[93]: the behavior of cadres elsewhere suggests that similar incentives were used in many places beginning in 1984.

Conclusion

In general, then, the relationship between private businesses and administrators improved as continued reforms took effect. Overt opposition and attacks on private business became less common, and the typical obstacles facing private businesses changed from the dead ends of limitation and blocking, to the expensive, but not insurmountable, problems of extortion and pay-offs. Although it has been argued here that there was a significant change after 1984, the widening of private business opportunities was not by any means a simple and discrete chronological progression. The dramatic, if temporary, drop in private business growth in 1986, and the fall in absolute numbers in 1989, are sufficient to illustrate that private business continued to be extremely vulnerable to policy fluctuations after 1984, in spite of the overall economic pressures for continued growth. Despite their continued political vulnerability, however, private businesses benefited from the economic pressures generated by reforms. This chapter discussed the changes these pressures brought about in administrative attitudes to, and treatment of, private businesses. The next chapter continues this story with a discussion of similar changes in the activities of private businesspeople, as they dealt with the practical problems of running their businesses and obtaining supplies, premises, and funding.

Notes

1. *RMRB*, 27 February 1983, p. 5.
2. *Beijing ribao* (Beijing Daily), 18 August 1980, quoted in *Beijing Review*, no. 45 (10 November 1980), p. 20.
3. Ren Zhonglin, "Guanyu geti jingji wenti," p. 19.
4. *Beijing Review*, no. 44 (2 November 1981), p. 27.
5. *Guangming ribao* (Enlightenment Daily, hereafter *GMRB*), 3 April 1983, p. 3.
6. *RMRB*, 7 January 1986, p. 2.
7. Lin Zili, ed., *Shehuizhuyi jingji lun*, p. 161.
8. Of course, by this time it was more difficult to start a private business: competition was fierce, premises expensive and hard to obtain, and it was commonly held that both bribes and good connections were necessary to obtain supplies. For an interesting report on the attitudes of young unemployed people and business operators in Chengdu in the late 1980s, see Ole Bruun, *Business and Bureaucracy in a Chinese City*, ch. 6.
9. Interview, Chengdu, September 1988.
10. In the mid-1980s 50–60 percent of registered private businesspeople came under this category, with variations in different localities. See Guowuyuan bangongting diaoyanshi, eds., *Geti jingji diaocha yu yanjiu*, for figures on Zhejiang, Guangdong, Shanghai, Nanjing, and Wuhan.
11. *RMRB*, 17 May 1987, p. 2.
12. *Zhongguo funü bao* (Chinese Women), 23 November 1987, p. 1; *Jingji ribao* (Economic Daily, hereafter *JJRB*), 26 November 1987, p. 1.
13. *RMRB*, 13 November 1988, p. 8.
14. For a further discussion of media presentation of *getihu*, see Thomas Gold, "Guerrilla Interviewing among the Getihu," p. 190.
15. See chapter 5.
16. *Nongmin ribao* (Peasants' Daily, hereafter *NMRB*), 16 December 1988, p. 2.
17. See, for example, the case of Wuxi county, Jiangsu, as described by Luo Xiaopeng in Byrd and Lin, eds., *China's Rural Industry*, p. 150.
18. Ibid., pp. 163, 199; Ole Odgaard, "The Success of Rural Enterprises in China," p. 69.
19. *Shichang* (The Market) editorial, quoted in *RMRB*, 28 March 1981, p. 2.
20. Solinger, *Chinese Business*, and "Commerce: The Petty Private Sector and the Three Lines in the Early 1980s," deals with this period in detail.

21. *RMRB*, 28 March 1981, p. 2.

22. See Cyril Lin, "Reinstatement of Economics," pp. 43–47.

23. See *GMRB*, 30 December 1983, p. 1; 4 January 1984, p. 1; and 9 January 1984, p. 1.

24. Yudkin, *Making Good*, p. 29.

25. *RMRB*, 20 May 1984, p. 3.

26. Meanwhile, reformists were quick to attack this interpretation, as illustrated by the August meeting referred to earlier, at which Hu Yaobang and other leaders received model *getihu* and emphasized in their speeches that individual business was both an honorable pursuit and good for the economy.

27. *JJRB*, 9 May 1984, p. 1; *RMRB*, 20 May 1984, p. 3.

28. "Guanyu fanshou fadong, zuzhi getihu jingying chaguan, chatan de tongzhi" (Notice on boldly encouraging and organizing individual operators to run teahouses and tea stalls), 13 August 1984, in *Siying he geti jingji shiyong fagui daquan*, pp. 154–55; see also *JJRB*, 22 August 1984, p. 1.

29. *RMRB*, 27 January 1983, p. 4.

30. *RMRB*, 27 February 1983, p. 5.

31. He and Zhu, "Geti jingji de fazhan"; Louise de Rosario, "The Private Dilemma."

32. He and Zhu, "Geti jingji de fazhan."

33. For example, *RMRB*, 1 August 1986, p. 2; 10 August 1986, p. 2; 24 September 1986, p. 2; and 27 September 1986, p. 2; *JJRB*, 11 November 1986, p. 1; and 22 November 1986, p. 2; Huang Zhongming, "Geti gongshanghu guanli zhong de falü wenti"; Ch'en Te-sheng, "'Individual Economy' in Mainland China," p. 10.

34. *ZTN*, 1990, p. 123.

35. See, for example, *RMRB*, 23 August 1986, p. 2; *JJRB*, 11 November 1986, p. 2.

36. Yudkin, *Making Good*, p. 83; *RMRB*, 29 June 1983, p. 1. The same tendency could be seen in 1989, when authorities in Shanghai decided to reduce the number of private taxis and not to allow any more wine bars, discos, coffee shops, etc. See *JJCK*, 16 March 1990, p. 2.

37. *Xinwen bao* (News), 10 March 1990, p. 1.

38. *Xinwen bao*, 10 March 1990, p. 1; *JJCK*, 5 February 1990, p. 2.

39. For example, *RMRB*, 2 November 1989, p. 2; *JJRB*, 2 August 1989, p. 1.

40. *SWB*, 25 October 1989, FE/0596 B2/8.

41. This figure is certainly unreliable as an indicator of the true situation. Some business operators handed in their licenses (or had them revoked), but still stayed in business; others managed to obtain the political protection of a collective license. Nevertheless, there was clearly a drop in private business operation in 1989.

42. *RMRB*, 29 June 1983, p. 1.

43. I am grateful to Ole Odgaard for this information.

44. Song Fangmin and Tan Lansheng, "Lai zi chengshi getihu de tiaozhan," p. 57.

45. Liu Long, ed., *Geti jingji yanjiu*, p. 114.

46. *RMRB*, 1 February 1986, p. 2; see also *RMRB*, 9 January 1982, p. 1; *RMRB*, 28 December 1986, p. 2.

47. *RMRB*, 27 February 1983, p. 5.

48. See the discussion of this question in Alec Nove, *The Economics of Feasible Socialism*, pp. 42–45.

49. Hu Guohua, Liu Jinghuai, and Chen Min, *Duo sediao de Zhongguo geti jingyingzhe*, p. 12.

50. Chao Yü-shen, "Expansion of Individual Economy," p. 9.

51. *JJRB*, 30 July 1984, p. 4.

52. *RMRB*, 10 July 1984, p. 2.

53. *RMRB*, 27 February 1983, p. 5.

54. See Ole Odgaard, "Collective Control of Income Distribution," p. 117.

55. *RMRB*, 7 July 1985, p. 2.

56. *RMRB*, 9 September 1984, p. 2.

57. Situ Shuqiang, "Geti jingying yu guoying shangdian jingzheng zhi wo jian," p. 23.

58. *RMRB*, 27 June 1987, p. 1; 30 June 1987, p. 1; 11 July 1987, p. 2.

59. *RMRB*, 27 June 1987, p. 1.

60. *RMRB*, 9 June 1984, p. 2; 20 June 1984, p. 2. For similar examples see *Ha'erbin ribao*, 28 March 1983, p. 1; *RMRB*, 24 January 1985, p. 1; *RMRB*, 27 July 1987, p. 2.

61. *RMRB*, 9 June 1984, p. 2; 20 June 1984, p. 2; *FBIS,* 2 August 1984, p. 3.

62. *JJRB*, 30 July 1984, p. 4.

63. Interview, Sichuan ICB cadre, August 1988.

64. He Wenfu, "Siying qiye fazhan mianlin de wenti."

65. *Zhongguo gongshang bao* (Chinese Industry and Commerce, hereafter *ZGGSB*), 3 August 1992, p. 1.

66. Odgaard, "Collective Control," p. 112.

67. *RMRB*, 19 February 1983, p. 2.

68. *RMRB*, 29 March 1983, p. 1.

69. *Ha'erbin ribao*, 4 January 1983, p. 1.

70. *RMRB*, 6 September 1987, p. 3. This argument was promoted, not so much to promote private enterprise as to deflect criticisms that the dismantling of collective agriculture had undone much of the progress China had made in providing basic health care to the rural population. According to *JJRB*, 23 December 1987, 30 percent of rural medical clinics were privately owned by that time.

71. *RMRB*, 20 July 1985, p. 5; 9 November 1988, p. 5; *JJRB*, 26 August 1987.

72. *RMRB*, 19 June 1985, p. 2.

73. *RMRB*, 27 July 1985, p. 2.

74. *JJCK*, 4 February 1989, p. 1.

75. *RMRB*, 19 July 1985, p. 4.

76. See also *RMRB*, 4 June 1985, p. 4; and 16 August 1985, p. 2.

77. *GMRB*, 31 August 1983, p. 1.

78. The Individual Laborers' Association (*Geti laodongzhe xiehui*) is the organization through which the government seeks to control private operators. Its role will be discussed further in chapter 6.

79. *RMRB*, 5 December 1986, p. 1.

80. Christopher Findlay and Andrew Watson, "Risk and Efficiency: Contracting in the Chinese Countryside," mimeo, University of Adelaide, February 1989, p. 16; see also Andrew Watson, "Investment Issues in the Chinese Countryside," pp. 98–99.

81. Jean C. Oi has developed this analysis in a number of articles, particularly "Fate of the Collective" and "Fiscal Reform and the Economic Foundations of Local State Corporatism in China." Andrew Watson emphasizes the relatively independent and self-interested nature of local governments under this system in "The Management of the Rural Economy," esp. pp. 177–82.

82. Unless their local economies appeared to be better served by restricting private sector development and promoting collective industry instead, as in the case of Wuxi county in Byrd and Lin, eds., *China's Rural Industry*.

83. Byrd and Lin, eds., *China's Rural Industry*; Ji Jianlin and Zhu Jun, "Siying qiye lirun liuxiang fenxi." Zhang Changyun, "Wo guo xiangzhen qiye suoyouzhi wenti yanjiu," gives an overview of different models of development under different conditions. The hypothesis that local governments in poorer regions will tend to be "predatory" toward enterprises is further developed in a review article by Dali L. Yang, "Local Government and Rural Industrialization in China."

84. Yudkin, *Making Good*, p. 29.

85. "Shanghai shi gongshangju guanyu fuchi chengzhen geti jingji ruogan wenti de buchong guiding" (Supplementary regulations of the Shanghai Bureau of Industry and Commerce on certain questions in supporting the urban individual economy), 15 May 1982, in Zhongguo shehui kexueyuan faxue yanjiusuo, eds., *Zhonghua renmin gongheguo jingji fagui xuanbian, 1982*, pp. 458–62.

86. Solinger, "Commerce," p. 79.

87. "Zhongong zhongyang, guowuyuan guanyu fazhan chengxiang lingshou shangye, fuwuye de zhibiao" (Central Committee and State Council guidelines on developing urban and rural retail and service industries), 5 March 1983, in Shangyebu bangongting, eds., *Shangye zhengce fagui huibian 1983*, pp. 3–10, p. 6.

88. "Zhongong zhongyang guanyu yi jiu ba si nian nongcun gongzuo de tongzhi" (Notice of the Central Committee concerning rural work in 1984), 1 January 1984, in Guojia gongshang xingzheng guanli ju geti jingji si and *Beijing ribao* lilun bu, eds., *Geti laodongzhe shouce*, pp. 188–201.

89. Published in *RMRB*, 12 March 1984, p. 4.

90. *RMRB*, 26 July 1984, p. 2.

91. *RMRB*, 19 October 1984, p. 2.

92. *RMRB*, 12 December 1984, p. 2.

93. Information provided by Andrew Watson.

——— 4 ———

Overcoming Material Constraints

The daily operations of private businesses were, of course, intimately affected by attitudes among officials, suppliers, and the community in general. The prejudices described earlier tended to aggravate the practical difficulties faced in an environment of high administrative involvement in business and limited resources. In many cases private operators suffered because they were small players in the new market economy created by the reforms, working within a framework set up for the planned economy. To this extent, the reformists' argument that the individual economy would be constrained and dominated by the state-run economy held true. Yet continuing reforms also changed relationships within the state-run economy and between it and private business, widening the opportunities open to private operators and making state bureaucrats and state enterprises more willing to deal with them. This chapter examines how these changes affected some of the major practical problems private businesses encountered.

Supplies

In the supply of goods, there is also a lot of unfairness toward individual businesses. Not only are the channels of supply few, but also what is assigned to individual businesses in the plan is often blocked off. Besides this, the tendency to supply only one's contacts is also quite serious in supplies.[1]

The main reason business has been bad for state shops is that they cannot compete with private enterprises in paying commissions. Individual businesses and private enterprises rely on bribes to buy goods in short supply, rely on giving presents to get out of paying taxes, and use policy loopholes to engage in profiteering.[2]

These quotations show two sides of the question of inputs for private businesses: one is the private operators' perennial complaint that obtaining supplies was even more difficult for them than for others, and the other gives the opposing view that the corruption rife in the Chinese economy made it all too easy for private operators to buy up goods and engage in profiteering. There is truth in both points of view. Obtaining supplies from state production or distribution units through official channels was often very difficult, even impossible, for private operators in the early years after 1978, and remained so for some commodities, especially raw materials. These problems were ameliorated by the effect of reforms, which made official channels easier and opened up many alternative sources of supply. Such was the nature of this supply system, however, with its uneasy mesh of planned and market distribution, inadequate distribution arrangements and pressing demand, that the opportunities for corruption were immense. To private businesses this meant that high-demand goods *could* be obtained—but at a price.

Obtaining inputs of raw materials, goods for resale, equipment, and energy was a constant problem for many private businesses. In June 1981 the ICB, Ministry of Commerce, Ministry of Food, the Supply and Marketing Cooperatives, and the Bureaus of Materials and Labor put out a joint notice on providing adequate supplies for individual businesses.[3] The notice expressed concern that, because of insufficient recognition of "the objective necessity of developing the urban individual economy," individual businesses were encountering problems in supplies, taxation, and excessive charges. The notice stipulated that, politically and economically, individual businesses should be treated as equal to state or collective units and given the wholehearted support of all departments. Local supply departments were to "actively supply" individual businesses, at the same wholesale prices enjoyed by state units. Yet the experiences of private operators differed greatly from this ideal.

Until the Chinese economy became more diversified as a result of reforms, private operators depended on state supply organs for the bulk of their goods or raw materials. The state wholesalers often discriminated against private buyers. This was attributed in press reports to the state units' inadequate grasp of the importance of the private economy or lingering leftist attitudes (i.e., opposition to the policy of encouraging private business) and to feelings of solidarity with state retailers threatened by private competition. The methods used against private businesses also indicate that in some cases state wholesalers discouraged individual buyers simply because their small orders were less convenient to handle than those of the larger state and collective buyers. These methods include charging private buyers the retail instead of the wholesale rate, refusing to sell in the small quantities private businesses wanted, selling high-quality goods only if accompanied by a consignment of poor quality, hard-to-sell goods, or simply refusing to sell to private businesses at all.[4] When commodities were in short supply, private businesses were the first to lose out: the response quoted in one press report of *getihu* supply problems was, "If we give everything to individual businesses, what will state workers eat? The wind?"[5] Private operators with only temporary licenses, such as those run by nonlocal residents, were not issued with tickets to buy supplies from wholesale departments.[6] In spite of government exhortations, state wholesalers often had neither the inclination to cater to private businesses nor any real incentive to do so.

The extreme difficulty of obtaining supplies has been noted as a feature common to the marginal private sectors of socialist economies. In China in the 1980s, however, a series of reforms in marketing worked to reduce the importance of state distribution agencies and to widen the supply avenues open to private business. For example in Hubei in 1983, over 95 percent of the goods sold by private retailers were bought from state commercial outlets and supply and marketing cooperatives. By 1987 this had fallen to 48.5 percent.[7] Private operators continued to be disadvantaged in many ways when obtaining supplies, but the nature of the problems they complained of changed. Until around 1984, private operators usually complained of outright refusal to sell them popular goods. In later years such complaints continued to appear, but they began to be far outnumbered by complaints that wholesalers took advantage of a seller's market by charging high prices and demanding bribes and favors. In these circumstances obtaining supplies might be difficult and would be expensive, but it could be done.

Free Markets

A major development in supply sources open to private businesses was the growth of the free markets, at first dealing in surplus and sideline agricultural produce and later expanding to include trading in a wide variety of commodities. The free markets began as an adjunct to the initial rural reforms, providing an outlet for peasants' surplus produce, but soon generated pressure for further developments such as long-distance trade and trade in nonagricultural products. Central Committee Document No. 1, 1983, on deepening rural reforms, advocated a greater role for free markets, and in February the State Council followed up with regulations on free markets that loosened restrictions on their operation, allowing state units, collectives and individuals to trade in unified and assigned purchase goods surplus to plan requirements.[8] The June 1983 regulations on the urban individual economy allowed individual businesses to engage in long-distance and wholesale trade and use mechanized vehicles. This central recognition and ratification of the role of free markets in turn gave further impetus to their growth.[9]

The free markets became important to private businesses, both as a source of supplies and as a venue for doing business. As the free market system developed, markets appeared dealing not only in agricultural and sideline products but in some of the raw materials needed by small private industry, such as scrap metal, waste products from state enterprises, and cloth.[10] Naturally, given the higher prices to be commanded at the free markets, some of the commodities supposed to be purchased under state plans were diverted to free markets instead. As specialized production and private business developed, there appeared wholesale markets devoted to particular commodities and patronized mainly by private traders buying goods either for resale or for their own manufacturing needs, although state and collective units of various kinds also participated.

One such market is the Beizhan market near the Chengdu railway station, administered by the district ICB. When I visited it in September 1988, three thousand-odd private stalls dealt here in clothing, knitting wool and cloth, and spices, and Chinese medicines. The stallholders bought the clothes mainly from yet other wholesale markets in Shanghai and Guangzhou, and they were sold at this market to individual traders who resold them at rural markets. The nearby Hehuachi market, which deals in industrial products and secondhand vehicles as well as the above commodities, had more than five thousand traders in 1990. In one day over six hundred private traders and sixteen state or collective units came from all over China to buy from the Chinese medicine section.[11] By 1993 the Beizhan and Hehuachi markets were part of one large trading area near the railway station, with designated stall spaces and shops whose holders included state, private, and collective enterprises from all over Sichuan. A market like this not only is a source of supplies for many private businesses but also provides new opportunities for private business to develop. It is an ideal start for would-be entrepreneurs with no capital, as they may begin by either simply working at a stall for good wages while the owner is off on buying trips, or running their own stall by selling on commission for larger traders, who specialize as middlemen in wholesale trade and long-distance transport.

Changes in State Unit Attitudes

At the same time as free markets were developing as an alternative source of supply, state units were being made more responsible for their profits. As a result their attitude to private operators often changed, and they were more likely to see them as potential sources of profit rather than merely as economic or ideological competitors. This resulted in wholesale departments becoming more willing to sell to individuals and expanding their services to set up branches aimed specifically at private businesses. The Xizang Trading Corporation, for example, realized in 1983 that Lhasa's more than one thousand eight hundred individual businesses were a market not to be sneezed at and began in February to sell to them at wholesale prices.[12] The participation of state units in the wholesale markets also showed a far greater interest in private customers, and the competition of the markets could sometimes lead to lower prices than individuals were formerly able to obtain. In 1987, one newspaper reporter visited a Hangzhou market where fifty-three state and township enterprises and more than one hundred individual traders sold silk products. Individual businesspeople interviewed told how they had formerly had to go all over Hangzhou visiting separate factories, and it was hard to be sure of getting the best price. They were now able to compare goods and prices on the spot, and bought more cheaply and more conveniently.[13]

Probably more important than the greater willingness of state suppliers to trade with private buyers through official channels was their willingness to trade unofficially. Goods in high demand were still hard for individuals to obtain officially, as the quota for individual businesses provided for in plans would be small or nonexistent, since they still came last in the traditional hierarchy of state, collective, and individual. Unofficially, however, the interest in profit-making created by the reforms meant that state production or distribution units might be willing to divert some of the materials they had obtained under state plans to individuals at high prices. In this way, for example, a tinsmith I interviewed in Chengdu in 1988 was able to buy imported sheet metal from Japan, which he could not otherwise have obtained. At times state units' preference for profitable sales to private buyers became so blatant that it left state and collective buyers unable to obtain goods. In Harbin in mid-1983, there was a dearth of bottled beer in state shops and restaurants. It turned out that the beer factory was selling some of its output outside the city, some direct to individual retailers and some to selected state shops, which, instead of retailing it to consumers, were reselling it to private restaurateurs, who resold it at 8 to 13 fen higher than the normal price.[14] In Changchun in the same year, the Changchun Fruit Products Corporation decided that, since a certain shipment of melons from Hainan was so small, none of these melons would be sold to private traders. But its supply station manager and party secretary had other ideas, and sold the melons to private traders and their own staff.[15] Such deals were sometimes more complicated, with one commodity being bartered for another. For example the Hangzhong district tobacco company in Jiangxi reportedly sold fifteen thousand cartons of cigarettes at wholesale price to two private traders, who then resold them to individual retailers; in return for this generosity the traders sold the company's famous-brand bicycles at a low price.[16]

In some cases the state unit or staff member would profit by selling not the commodities themselves but the state-unit status that facilitates buying. Many of the cases of illegal trading reported in the media involved individual businesspeople using checks, identification, or letters of introduction from state or collective units.[17] These were sometimes forged, but they could also be obtained with the collaboration of cadres in the unit concerned, in return for a cut of the proceeds.

Illegal sales could be made by the management of state units, or by staff members lower down. Cigarettes, for example, were often sold in small quantities by individuals on their own account. In either case, it was necessary for private traders to have good connections with the people concerned. Private businesspeople interviewed in 1988, 1992, and 1993 consistently listed good connections as one of the main prerequisites for success in business, particularly in obtaining supplies. Private businesses in trades where supplies might be expected to be a problem, such as a tinsmith, a signmaker using plastics, and a chicken farmer requiring large amounts of feed, were run by former state employees or their relatives, and obtained their materials from their former work units or from connections made when working there. The problem for most private businesses was that if they did not happen to have these connections, they had to be bought. (One private operator I spoke to, however, commented that these days even if you did have connections, they still expected to be paid.) High demand for some goods provided ample opportunity for cadres and enterprise staff who had power over those goods to profit from their position. "If you want to get some goods through a state unit, you have to give big presents. A few years ago it was no problem for us to get some clothes wholesale from the Foreign Trade Bureau wholesale department, but now unless you give presents, you won't get one piece," complained the operator of a clothing stall in 1984.[18]

Thus although the channels for obtaining supplies increased, such goods were expensive and, for many businesses, still by no means easy to get. Good connections were particularly important to the larger enterprises, since they tended to need greater quantities of a wider variety of inputs. Of fifty-four rural private enterprises surveyed in Shanxi in 1988, 53 percent bought their raw materials in free markets easily, but complained at the price; 20 percent got supplies through connections, and still at high prices; and 5.8 percent said they often had trouble obtaining materials, to the point of having to suspend production because they lacked inputs.[19] The enterprises, whose average gross profit was around 80,000 yuan, found that they had to spend an average of 10,000 yuan on cultivating connections; some spent as much as 30,000 yuan.[20] One entrepreneur commented that every road had many "wealth gods," to whom offerings had to be made if doors were to be opened and business continued.[21]

One consequence of the difficulty of obtaining supplies and

the importance of connections is the rise of a new group of private traders who operate specifically as brokers, using their market knowledge and connections to obtain goods for which enterprises, both private and otherwise, will pay high prices. They are a freelance version of the buyers used by state enterprises both before the reforms, to overcome shortfalls in the planning system, and after the reforms to represent their enterprise in the marketplace. They may both cooperate and compete with their counterparts in state units. In Wenzhou, with its thriving private enterprise, these brokers are called "worker bees" and are an important link in the operation of the economy. Such people may buy and sell goods on their own behalf or act as brokers for a commission.[22] By 1988 the latter arrangement was also a common part-time money-raiser for virtually anyone in Chinese society who happened to know the right people at the right time. At the shadier end of this kind of dealing were the illegal traders known as *daoye*, who used connections to buy up goods such as famous-brand wines and cigarettes, grain, fertilizer, televisions, even special-issue postage stamps, for resale at high prices.[23] With time, the illicit trade in some items became quite regular and open. In Chengdu, for example, there was a regular cigarette market on the banks of the Jin River, where private vendors could buy top-brand cigarettes at about twice the state retail price. In August 1987 this market was reported as handling two thousand to three thousand cartons each day; one year later it was still going strong, and several private vendors I spoke to said they always got their top-brand cigarettes there.[24] The area became known as one that police could be relied on to leave pretty much alone. In the latter half of 1987 the issue of *daoye* was canvassed extensively in the national press as a campaign against speculation and profiteering was launched. The ICB was anxious to make a clear distinction between *daoye* and law-abiding, licensed private traders.[25] However, the difficulty of obtaining supplies of some commodities through legitimate channels meant that an unbroken, if convoluted, line of mutual dependence often connected the state supply station cadre, one or more licensed or unlicensed go-betweens, and the private retailer. This is one of the reasons why the private sector was seen by some in China as a major—even *the* major—cause of increasing corruption, as it was the outlet for illegally obtained goods and its operation provided myriad opportunities for bribery and extortion.[26]

Space for Business Premises

A more severe constraint on the growth of private businesses in China than the problem of supplies was that of finding business premises. Here again, private businesspeople were disadvantaged because of their political insecurity and low status and their lack of institutional backing. In an effort to make private businesses more manageable, ICB departments would often not issue a license unless fixed premises had been arranged. In Shanghai in mid-1986, more than two thousand applicants were unable to obtain their licenses for this reason, and lack of premises was commonly cited by both administrators and private operators as one of the major impediments to further development of the private economy.[27] One way in which state units have been known to attack private businesses is to hold an "environment beautification campaign" and demand that private stalls near their premises be removed for aesthetic reasons.[28] It has been noted that this concern for appearances is purely discriminatory and reserved for the ugliness of private stalls, vehicles, or signs alone.[29] Although central government departments took steps to have space for private businesses included in city planning as early as May 1981,[30] local departments often saw private businesses as unsightly, disruptive of public order, and an impediment to traffic.

> Some cities have specific regulations forbidding individual stalls from busy streets, and the sites opened up for trading markets are always in remote places, where there is no business to be done. Because many districts have not included the question of premises for individual businesses in city construction plans, individual businesses are often moved from one place to another.[31]

In 1984, a group of private stallholders wrote to *Renmin ribao* complaining of just such a problem.[32] In March 1983, their marketplace had been burned down in a fire started in a nearby apartment building. They expected to move into the replacement building nine months later, but were then told that the market was a fire hazard and would be banned. In March 1984, public security personnel broke up the market and removed the stalls. The newspaper followed up a month after the letter with an article saying that cadres should "give the green light" to collective and private business in order to provide jobs and held up an example from Lanzhou, where stalls and marketplaces had been built especially for private traders.[33]

Lanzhou was not alone in this. As ICB departments, responding to policy directives, began to look for ways to promote private business, they began to see the advantages of setting up such marketplaces. The first noticeable result of this was the appearance in Chinese streets of rows of more permanent stalls, usually in green roofing sheets, tin, or wood, which could be locked at night. These often developed from a spontaneous gathering of private stalls and were usually set up by the ICB in consultation with street committees and departments such as traffic and city planning, and then rented out to individual businesspeople. In this way the businesspeople got more permanent, weatherproof premises, and the ICB or the street committee got both the rent and the administrative advantage of having regular stallholders in one spot. This often resulted in the development of very successful markets. The many underground air-raid shelters in China's cities were also used in this way. In the Sichuan industrial city of Zigong, the ICB used administration fees collected from individual businesses to turn an air-raid tunnel into the Nongchang Market in 1984. In September 1988 the market had 349 businesses, mainly private, each paying 30–50 yuan rent per month per stall (some businesses had more than one stall), plus another 30–40 yuan in fees and electricity charges. The stalls were in high demand: if a stallholder left, he or she could charge up to 3,000 yuan for handing the stall over to another operator.[34] A thriving night market I visited in Guangzhou was set up in a similar way: stallholders arrived each evening to set up stalls on numbered spaces on the road. They had bought their own stall-building materials to ICB specifications; the ICB had only to pay for the spaces to be painted and electrical wiring to be installed for lighting. The demand for these stalls was far from being met, and there was an unofficial market in stall-spaces that were sold or sublet for large sums.

These organized markets had both advantages and disadvantages from the point of view of private business. Permanent, weatherproof stalls, especially the type with a small, lockable storage space at the back, were an advantage to stallholders, and the concentration of stalls attracted customers. On the other hand, such markets were sometimes another manifestation of the government desire to collect private businesses in one place, where market control officials and tax collectors could keep an eye on them and where they would be off the streets.[35]

Stall-space, while by no means easy, was not too difficult to find, as stalls are small and cheap to set up. One could always begin by just setting up at the side of the road, keeping a wary eye out for ICB officials. Larger, more permanent premises were more of a problem, especially in crowded cities. In Chengdu, a family who happened to own one of the old, two-story timber houses fronting a busy street need never work again. They could simply rent out the ground floor of one or two rooms. A small shop of some eight square meters could be rented for 50–200 yuan per month in 1988, depending on its location. Lease agreements were often intentionally informal or unclear, if landlords wished to mislead taxation or other officials. For example a shop rented from the state at a low rent of 2 yuan per square meter might be sublet officially at the low rate, with the remainder of the market rate paid separately. Extra rent was sometimes further disguised by listing the landlord or a relative as an employee receiving "wages."[36] In Chengdu, rents had risen rapidly before 1988, so that landlords were often unwilling to give long leases, and had been known to break leases in order to move in a new tenant at a higher rent. This made even those private operators who had obtained rented premises insecure, as landlords might wish to raise the rent beyond their tenants' means, or, alternatively, take up business themselves. Entrepreneurs who owned or had relatives who owned suitable premises had no problem, and some operators managed to buy premises. A two-story, two- or three-room older-style house in Chengdu sold for around 10,000 yuan in 1986, and for at least twice as much in 1988.

In Beijing, prices were much higher. A clothing retailer whom I interviewed on Wangfujing Street had rented his shop of about 24 square meters from the struggling state hairdressers' in 1985, for 2,500 yuan per month. By 1988 the rent was 3,600 yuan. In 1984 the owners of a thriving restaurant behind the Beijing Hotel paid 3,000 yuan per month for their restaurant of three good-sized rooms and a sleeping room upstairs. When their restaurant proved successful, the state unit owning the shop asked for a fifty–fifty split of the profits instead. Of course the businesses in both of these examples, being in Beijing's main commercial street, must have been paying among the highest rents in town.

Productive enterprises, needing larger workshops or factories and access to transport, and energy supplies, had more difficulty finding premises than shops and restaurants. During the 1980s city planning authorities were often unwilling to allow further industrial development in heavily populated areas; the thrust of planning policies was to promote new industry in outlying small towns, where it could simultaneously promote economic development in rural areas and absorb some of the surplus labor and capital released by rural reforms. In rural areas and smaller towns, premises could usually be arranged, although county- and village-level officials sometimes used their power over land-use decisions to demand a share in the profits or other benefits, in addition to rent, in return for providing space.[37] Even without such considerations, however, the reforms to local government budgeting created strong incentives for local cadres to encourage private enterprises in order to increase local revenue and employment. This meant that a private investor whose enterprise showed

promise of succeeding was likely to find local cadres quite ac-
commodating when it came to leasing or buying space for the
enterprise. Thus the Sichuan chicken producer mentioned earlier
was able to lease a total of around 50 *mu* (1 *mu* = approximately
1/6 acre) of land from the village-level administration on a
twenty-year lease at around 540 yuan per *mu* per year.[38] On the
other hand, many observers have noted that the process of gaining the required approvals remained very complicated and bureaucratic. An alternative was to use one's own private plot, the
use of which was left more to a family's own discretion.[39]

Long-term leases were approved in the changes made to the rural
land contracting system in Central Committee Document No. 1
of 1984, as the former three-year contracts were found to discourage investment in and proper use of the land. A more permanent way of obtaining land was to *zheng di*, that is, to buy the
right to use the land.[40] In such arrangements the use of the land
was transferred, more or less permanently in many cases, in return for a once-only lump sum payment. In this way private
enterprises were able to obtain land by making deals with the
collective or, more rarely, state-unit "owners" of the land, sometimes even in urban areas. One enterprise I visited in a county on
the outskirts of Chengdu had obtained five factory sites, either by
leasing from the county administration or by simply buying existing buildings outright. In Sichuan, prices seemed surprisingly
low: one private enterprise had been renting a well-appointed
two-story factory and offices in Chengdu itself from the city
construction department for 20,000 yuan per year, but was about
to move to a new, less central site for a one-time payment of
around 30,000 yuan.[41] A 1988 Chinese article reports one-time
land-use fees of 5,000 to 10,000 yuan per *mu* in Changle county
in Fujian.[42] Aiguo Lu and Mark Selden, in a 1987 article on land
ownership, found much higher prices elsewhere, particularly for
urban and suburban land.[43] The transferal of use-rights, notion-
ally different from ownership rights, was legalized in the revi-
sions made to the constitution by the seventh National People's
Congress in April 1988, but such transferals appear to have been

common well before this. Unfortunately, documentation of specific arrangements is difficult to find, as they were often private deals of mutual benefit between the entrepreneur and the unit in charge of the land, kept fairly quiet because of their dubious legal standing.

Although premises remained expensive and difficult to obtain in urban areas, as might be expected in a country as crowded as China, the economic changes brought about by reforms helped ease the situation here too. Urban authorities were aware that the economic advantages of promoting private enterprise, such as increased revenue, increased employment, and better services to consumers, could not be obtained unless the logistical problems of private businesses were solved. As a result, some city planning departments, in conjunction with the ICB and the Labor Bureau, did begin to provide space for private business. It was reported that by 1986 Jinan had provided premises for over four thousand eight hundred businesses, and loans totaling 14 million yuan, in order to increase employment opportunities.[44] The ICB's sponsorship of marketplaces for private stalls, described above, was also part of this change, as it could not take place without the collaboration of city planning and local government authorities.

Private businesses installed in older buildings were often the casualties of the massive reconstruction going on in Chinese cities in the 1980s. If a private operator was compensated and found alternative premises, this could be an advantage, as in these circumstances rents were usually low. Zhang Guangyi, a "model" individual pen repairer in Beijing, used to own premises that were knocked down to make way for new construction. In 1988, as a result, he was renting a shop from the state for a laughable 10 yuan per month.[45] Other private operators, however, sometimes complained that they were moved out without alternative provisions or adequate compensation, especially if their premises were in a good location.[46] Given the potential for rental income of any privately owned building in a busy area, compensation for the change from proprietor to tenant would have to be high indeed to be truly adequate.

The economic reforms also encouraged the building of new commercial premises, however. In many cases the older-style wooden buildings, admirably suited to small private commercial businesses as operators could both live and work in them, were replaced by large multistory apartment blocks. But the organizations building these blocks were generally not blind to the economic advantages of renting out commercial premises, and the ground floor of newer buildings is very often divided into shops that private businesses can rent.

The pressure on state and collective units to be responsible for their own profits and losses was also of benefit to private business in this way, as unsuccessful units sometimes found it easier simply to rent out their premises, or a part of them, to private businesses, as did the state hairdressers' on Wangfujing Street mentioned earlier. State department stores began to lease out individual counters to private operators, often for higher rents than their former sales income; for example, a department store in Yinchuan city, Ningxia, rented out twelve counters for a total of over 12,000 yuan per month, roughly equivalent to the profit on nineteen counters it operated.[47] One private clothes-seller interviewed at the store said that although the rent was high, conditions were much better than in the outdoor market and his clothes did not get damaged by the weather. Some of his colleagues said that the rent of 1,000 to 1,500 yuan a month was too high, and they would move out once winter was over. In existing stores local authorities often limited the number of counters allowed to be rented out, but in Chengdu, new buildings appeared after 1985 that were built with renting specifically in mind. A new building in the outer-city shopping area of Shahe, for example, devoted its ground floor to small counters, each of which was rented to individual traders for 250 to 300 yuan per month in 1988.[48]

Finance

From the early stages of the policy of promoting private business, certain attempts were made at a government level to provide private entrepreneurs with financial assistance. The People's Bank began in 1980 to give loans to individual businesses with sufficient collateral or a guarantor. Initially, loans were limited to under 1,000 yuan, but local branches gradually increased the limit.[49] Article 10 of the State Council's 1981 regulations on the urban individual economy stated that local governments and relevant departments such as the ICB and the Labor Bureau could make arrangements to provide financial assistance to individual businesses whose funds were insufficient; in addition, it confirmed that individual businesses could also apply for bank loans. Obtaining such loans appears to have been a little easier in rural areas, especially after 1984. The Agricultural Bank announced in July 1984 that it would give loans to private operators more easily, and the lending guidelines it circulated in December allowed borrowing by a wide range of business types.[50] The Industrial and Commercial Bank followed suit, making loans available for the first time to the more mobile transport, tourism, and household repair businesses, and allowing loans for the purchase of vehicles.[51] Such official sources of funding remained extremely limited, however, and often ill-suited to the circumstances and requirements of individual businesses. Bank loans were short term, usually for three to six months, and the guarantor generally had to be a state or collective unit of reasonable standing. It was often impossible, particularly in the early years after 1978, when suspicion of and opposition to private business was widespread, for an individual operator to obtain such a guarantor. Banks, too, remained much less helpful to private businesses than central-level documents might suggest; some branches would not even let individual businesses open accounts.[52] If they did, to open an account as an economic entity required extensive checks and perhaps a larger, state, or collective umbrella unit, while a normal individual savings account did not offer services like credit transfers.[53] Interviewees in China suggested that the state-run banks, used to dealing within the planned, collective economy, often saw private businesses, with their unreliable accounting and small transactions, as more trouble than they were worth.

In fact, although press reports appeared criticizing the unhelpful attitude of banks toward private businesses, the antipathy was often mutual. The majority of private entrepreneurs preferred to keep at least some, if not all, of their funds in cash for several reasons. A major motive was to keep one's true financial position secret from government officials, both to avoid taxes and in case of a reversal of policies supporting private business. Another important reason was that banks, in the tradition of dealing with state units whose funds belonged to the state, tended to refuse to allow large cash withdrawals; it was, private businesspeople said, much easier to get money into the bank than to get it out again.[54] Cash transactions were also preferred over checks or credit transfers for tax reasons, because goods could be bought cheaper for cash and because bank transactions were often too slow or inadequate for the needs of private businesses. For example, checks do not appear to have become available to private businesses until 1986, involved fairly complicated identification procedures, and were normally for use only within one municipality and therefore useless to a large number of private traders dealing across long distances.[55] As a result, private businesspeople were accustomed to carrying huge amounts of cash, sometimes tens of thousands, when on buying trips, thus providing a growing source of income for that other thriving post-reform industry, transit robbery. In the Hehuachi wholesale market in Chengdu, 90 percent of the 1988 turnover was reported to have been in cash transactions, and thirteen private traders investigated at the market averaged over 150,000 yuan in cash holdings at the end of 1988.[56]

Although funds from official sources remained limited, alternative finance became increasingly available as reforms opened up the economy. The majority of smaller businesses were started with personal or family savings or loans from relatives and friends, and the high profitability of private business meant that large amounts of capital could be built up from small beginnings. Loans also became available from new collective banks and credit societies set up by a variety of units, and at high interest from unofficial credit societies and private individuals.

Many private businesses, such as repairs or roadside stalls, needed very little starting capital. The few tens or hundreds of yuan needed for license fees (if a license was obtained), tools, a shelter, and the first consignments of goods were well within the reach of the average family. But larger businesses, too, could be developed from similarly small beginnings. The proprietor of a bakery whom I interviewed in Chengdu in 1988, was originally a worker in a collective unit on a salary of some 40 yuan per month. His family had been in business before 1949, and he was quick to see the opportunities offered by reform policies. In 1984 he applied to leave his job, but his unit would not release him. He left anyway and, being unable to obtain a license without his unit's release, did business unlicensed for two years. He started out in a small way, selling beef that he bought from peasants. Then he switched to fruit, going out to buy a load of fruit and selling it in the city. By 1986, when his unit finally agreed to release him, he was able to invest 12,000 yuan, nearly all his own, in setting up his bakery and shop. A woman who ran a clothing business that had a turnover of some 4 million yuan in 1987 told a similar story. She too used to work in a state factory, but left in 1983 because the factory's leaders, zealous about the birth control campaign, were making her life difficult after her decision to have her one child outside the factory's quota. With a few hundred yuan, she started a stall selling clothing in Chengdu's Beizhan market, getting up early to go and buy the clothes. Later, as she started to build up a little capital, she bought clothes from Shanghai, still later establishing links with well-known Shanghai clothing factories. By 1988 she had her own factory making 50 percent of the goods she sold, plus a shop in the city, a warehouse and four stalls in the Beizhan market, and admitted to fixed assets of 800,000 yuan. By this time, she was able to get substantial loans from a collectively owned bank, and she thought her next project, if only she could find the land, might be a hotel/office building in the city. I was unable to interview her on a return visit in 1993, but her business still appeared to be doing well and now included a karaoke bar and a small taxi company.

Small retail, repair, or catering businesses were a popular start for individuals with limited funds. Those without even the funds to set up a stall could start out by running a stall on commission. Many of the stallholders in the Beizhan market had started in this way. The stallholder was responsible for market and license fees, while a distributor supplied the clothes. Mr. Liu, a stallholder in the market who, like most of his colleagues, admitted to liquid assets of 40,000 yuan in 1988 (although as mentioned above, the operators of similar stalls in the Hehuachi market nearby were reported to be worth three times as much), had started by working for wages at a stall run by someone else. Then he got his own stall, but sold on commission because he lacked the funds to get his own supplies. By 1988, he was employing two people to run the stall, while he devoted his time to making buying trips to Shanghai and Fujian, cultivating connections, and reading about foreign entrepreneurs and the privatization policies of Margaret Thatcher, which he followed with great interest and approval.

It was clearly possible, therefore, for successful private businesses to be started in the 1980s from the kind of funds an average family could provide. Many private businesses were also launched with help from relatives and friends, raising the start-up capital to several thousand yuan—sufficient to start up a permanent workshop or retail business. Among the private businesspeople I interviewed in 1988, loans of this sort were far more common than loans from other sources.

Other sources were available, however, although often at very high rates of interest. After 1985 the Chinese financial system was loosened up and many small financial banks and credit societies appeared, serving mainly collective and private enterprises. An example is the Huitong Urban Collective Bank in Chengdu. Set up by the Southwest Finance University and other state units in 1985, by 1988 its shareholders also included some individuals.[57] According to the manager any licensed private business could open an account, and the whole balance could be freely withdrawn in cash. Loans were available to private businesses at state-regulated rates: before September 1988 the rate was between 0.93

and 0.99 percent per month for private businesses, as opposed to 0.9 percent for collectives. After September when the government raised interest rates, the rates rose to 1.35 percent per month and 1.2 percent per month respectively. Loans were generally for three to six months, but could be renegotiated at the end of that time. First loans for private businesses were usually from 30,000 to 60,000 yuan, but once the enterprises had built up more mortgageable assets larger loans were possible: the manager gave the example of a million-yuan loan made to the Chengdu clothing company, mentioned earlier. Pawn shops and credit cooperatives also reappeared in major cities, catering to private and collective businesses.[58]

In many rural areas private moneylending re-emerged and became common. In some cases those who had obtained loans from state banks and credit societies then re-lent all or part of the money to others at higher interest. For example, an individual transporter who borrowed 40,000 yuan in 1985 was reported to have lent the money to three peasants to start a business. They were to pay back the principal plus the bank rate of interest, plus a share of the profits.[59] Private money-lending institutions formed by groups of individuals became common and were often organized along similar lines to traditional banks or credit unions. There were also revolving credit societies in which members pooled funds, then took turns in borrowing. One survey found that over 30 percent of all rural households were involved in some form of private money-lending.[60] In Wenzhou in 1986, it was estimated that the unofficial finance market was providing over 200 million yuan annually, about 30 percent of the capital required by township enterprises.[61] Loans between family members were usually interest-free; loans between friends sometimes carried about the same interest as if the money were deposited in a bank account.[62] Other loans were usually at very high interest rates, even as high as 40 percent per month.[63] A survey of rural borrowers in Jiangsu found that over 20 percent were borrowing at unspecified "high interest."[64] In Chengdu in 1990, the private lending rate was generally 3.5 to 4.5 percent per month.[65] These high rates reflect not only a high demand for funds, but also the high profitability of private business ventures. Borrowers were expected, and indeed were usually able, to pay back the loans within a few months, and according to the Jiangsu report quoted above, the amounts borrowed were increasing from a few hundred yuan to thousands. Reports in 1989, however, suggested that in some areas nongovernment credit institutions were overreaching themselves; in Wenzhou in early 1989, no doubt at least partly as a result of the centrally initiated credit squeeze, more than twenty such institutions failed with liabilities exceeding 1 million yuan.[66]

Thus it can be seen that in the latter half of the 1980s, the financial arrangements open to private entrepreneurs became extremely diverse. Both the state banks, and the collective banks from 1985 onward, improved the financial services available to private businesses, and loans became much more freely, if expensively, available from a wide variety of sources. The banking system, however, remained far from adequate to the demands of the dynamic commercial economy of the private traders, and this combined with their distaste for taxation and distrust of officialdom to make the majority steer clear of official financial institutions.

Conclusion

This chapter has examined the ways in which private businesses solved problems in three common areas: supplies, premises, and finance. The three show a common pattern. In each of them, central policy support was echoed, more slowly, by changes at lower levels of the administrative hierarchy. The slack left by inadequate official responses was taken up to some degree by the much more readily adaptable solutions that arose from the changing economic situation. Thus as the reform process progressed a stage was reached at which it began to generate its own solutions. Private businesses both benefited from this and contributed to it. Both administrative cadres and state production and distribution units became more willing to deal with private businesses either legitimately or otherwise. This economic dynamism had further consequences for the subsequent path of reform.

With increased attention to profitability, state enterprises became weary of their burden of excess employees, adding further impetus to the generation of private employment as an alternative. The increased role of the market and the preferability of market sales made it yet more difficult for state planning to function, as goods were diverted to the free market. A similar trend can be seen in the evolution of the land and capital markets. The unofficial nature of the responses to economic opportunities in the areas discussed in this chapter led to similar consequences in each case: high prices and corruption in supplies; an impenetrable legal minefield in the realm of land ownership; and high interest, lack of government monetary control, and speculation in the field of finance. An uneasy and shifting combination of state, state-approved, private, unofficial, and downright illegal arrangements evolved—one that seemed in many instances to be lubricated by the widespread corruption that became one of the major political and economic problems facing the Chinese government in the late 1980s.

The economic pressures generated by the reforms were favorable to the growth of private enterprise, and the responses to these pressures began to challenge long-held concepts concerning the proper hierarchical distribution of the state, the collective, and the individual and the role of the government in the economy. This section has discussed the interaction among private businesspeople, cadres, and other enterprises, and how this interaction was affected by the reform process. The following chapters will discuss these changes in relation to three issues: the changing role and nature of the private economy in China, the administrative problems arising from these changes, and finally the consequent moves to reassess both the private sector and China's approach to ownership issues as a whole.

Notes

1. *RMRB*, 28 December 1988, p. 2.
2. State shop manager, *RMRB*, 4 April 1988, p. 2.
3. Guojia gongshang xingzheng guanli ju, shangye bu, liangshi bu,

gongxiao hezuoshe, guojia wuzi zongju, and guojia laodong zongju, "Guanyu dui chengzhen geti gongshangyehu huoyuan gongying deng wenti de tongzhi" (Notice on supplies to urban individual businesses and related problems), 22 June 1981, in Guojia gongshang xingzheng guanli ju geti jingji si and *Beijing ribao* lilun bu, eds., *Geti laodongzhe shouce*, pp. 42–43.

4. For example, see *RMRB*, 5 July 1981, p. 5; 9 January 1983, p. 1; *Zhongguo nongmin bao* (Chinese Peasant News), 4 September 1983; *RMRB*, 7 February 1985, p. 7. Solinger, "Commerce," p. 93, describes this kind of problem in detail. The same problems have been noted by students of the private economy in Eastern Europe; see Andors Åslund, "The Functioning of Private Enterprise in Poland," p. 432.

5. *RMRB*, 3 May 1984, p. 7.

6. Zhang Caiqing, "Guoying shangye yingdang zhichi geti shangye de shidang fazhan," p. 60.

7. Huang Chengxi, "Guoying shangye zhudao zuoyong jiantui de yuanyin ji duice," pp. 14–15.

8. State Council, "Chenxiang jishi maoyi guanli banfa" (Procedures for the administration of trade in free markets), 5 February 1983, in *Ha'erbin ribao*, 24 February 1983, p. 4.

9. Andrew Watson, "The Reform of Agricultural Marketing in China since 1978."

10. Ibid.

11. ICB report obtained at an interview, Chengdu, January 1991.

12. *RMRB*, 11 February 1983, p. 2.

13. *JJCK*, 18 December 1987, p. 1.

14. *Ha'erbin ribao*, 14 June 1983, p. 2; 24 June 1983, p. 2; 17 July 1983, p. 2.

15. *Ha'erbin ribao*, 29 June 1983, p. 4.

16. *NMRB*, 1 January 1988, p. 3.

17. For examples see *Ha'erbin ribao*, 17 September 1983, p. 2; *RMRB*, 13 February 1984, p. 1; *JJRB*, 10 March 1987, p. 3.

18. *RMRB*, 4 April 1984, p. 2.

19. *NMRB*, 16 December 1988, p. 2; *RMRB*, 25 December 1988, p. 8.

20. Ibid. See also Hu, Liu, and Chen, *Duo sediao de Zhongguo geti jingyingzhe*, p. 161.

21. *NMRB*, 16 December 1988, p. 2.

22. See Tao Youzhi, "Luelun geti jingji de zhengdun yu fazhan," p. 23; Li Fan et al., "Shanghai xiao shangpin shichang geti shangfan jingying qingquang yu jiaqiang guanli de yijian," p. 78.

23. *RMRB*, 16 August 1987, p. 2; *JJRB*, 14 August 1987, p. 1; 7 September 1987, p. 1.

24. See *RMRB*, 26 August 1987, p. 1.

25. *RMRB*, 16 August 1987, p. 2; *JJRB*, 26 August 1987, p. 1.

26. Gregory Grossman describes a similar network of connections between the private economy, officialdom, and organized crime in the Soviet Union in "Sub-Rosa Privatization and Marketization in the USSR," p. 50.

27. See the reports by municipal and provincial authorities in Guowuyuan bangongting diaoyan shi, eds., *Geti jingji*, esp. p. 36 regarding Shanghai.

28. Tong Haosheng and Xu Gang, "You zheyang yihuo nianqing ren," p. 21.

29. *RMRB*, 9 January 1982; 9 November 1985, p. 5; 3 April 1986, p. 7.

30. On 6 May 1981, the State Labor Bureau, State Bureau of Urban Construction, the Bureau of Public Security, and the Bureau of Industry and Commerce put out a "Notice on solving the problem of space for the urban collective economy and individual economy"; reproduced in Guojia gongshang xingzheng guanli ju geti jingji si and *Beijing ribao* lilun bu, eds., *Geti laodongzhe shouce*, pp. 44–45.

31. *RMRB*, 28 December 1986, p. 2.

32. *RMRB*, 14 July 1984, p. 5.

33. *RMRB*, 11 August 1984, p. 5.

34. Interview, Zigong, September 1988.

35. Solinger, "Commerce," pp. 86–87, gives a good example of this from two 1982 press reports: in Lanzhou, the concentration of private stalls in controlled areas was praised, whereas the same phenomenon in Ha'rbin was criticized as obviating the benefits to consumers of scattered, flexible private shops.

36. See *JJRB*, 2 August 1987, p. 2.

37. *NMRB*, 16 December 1988, p. 2.

38. Interview, September 1988.

39. Ole Odgaard, personal communication.

40. I am grateful to Li Qingzeng for answering questions on this subject for me.

41. Interview, September 1988.

42. Chen Jianhua, "Cong wu xu dao you xu."

43. Aiguo Lu and Mark Selden, "The Reform of Land Ownership and the Political Economy of Contemporary China," pp. 240, 243.

44. *RMRB*, 7 January 1986, p. 2.

45. Interview, August 1988. No doubt his rent was influenced by his "model" status and the fact that repair shops like his were seen as highly desirable by the authorities.

46. *RMRB*, 28 December 1986, p. 2; He and Zhu, "Geti jingji de fazhan," p. 8; Ole Bruun, "The Reappearance of the Family as an Economic Unit," p. 125.

47. *RMRB*, 23 February 1988, p. 1.

48. Interview, September 1988. In 1989 several articles were published criticizing the leasing of counters by state enterprises on the grounds that there was little or no control of the private operators' business practices and that consumers, lulled into a false sense of security because they were shopping in a state store, were being cheated. In Shenyang, state shops were banned from leasing counters to private operators. See *JJCK*, 1 March 1989, p. 2, and 3 July 1989, p. 2; Liu Guanglu, "Guoying, jiti shangye chuzu guitai qingquang de diaocha."

49. Hu, Liu, and Chen, *Duo sediao de geti jingyingzhe*, p. 7.

50. "Zhongguo nongye yinhang nongcun geti gongshangye daikuan shi-xing banfa" (Agricultural Bank of China trial procedures for loans to individual industrial and commercial households), *Zhongguo jinrong nianjian* (Financial Yearbook of China), 1986, p. 58.

51. *JJRB*, 29 January 1985, p. 2.

52. Solinger, *Chinese Business*, p. 203.

53. Much of the information in the following discussion was obtained from interviews with private businesspeople and academics in Beijing and Chengdu in 1988. I am particularly indebted to Wang Shihua of the Sichuan Academy of Social Sciences and Yuan Yong of the Huitong Urban Collective Bank.

54. Information from interviews, 1988. See *JJCK*, 28 May 1989, p. 2; *SWB*, 25 October 1989, FE/0596 B2/8.

55. *RMRB*, 19 April 1986, p. 4; 10 August 1986, p. 2.

56. *JJCK*, 28 May 1989, p. 2.

57. Interview, Chengdu, September 1988.

58. *SWB*, 7 January 1989, FE/0352 B2/7; *Shoudu jingji xinxi bao* (Capital Economic News), 23 February 1988, p. 1.

59. *NMRB*, 24 February 1986, p. 4.

60. *Zhongguo cunzhen baiye xinxi bao* (China Village Trades Informer), 14 January 1987, p. 1, cited in Watson, "Investment Issues," p. 108.

61. Zhang Renshou, Yang Xiaoguang, and Lin Dayue, " 'Wenzhou moshi' dui jingji tizhi gaige de xiangdao yiyi," p. 7.

62. *Zhongguo shangbao* (China Commercial News), 18 March 1989, p. 1.

63. Watson, "Investment Issues," p. 107.

64. *Zhongguo shangbao*, 18 March 1989, p. 1.

65. Chengdu ICB report obtained at an interview, Chengdu, January 1991.

66. *Xinwen bao* (News), 11 April 1989, p. 1.

——— 5 ———

Changes in the Private Sector

The impact of the post-1978 reforms on attitudes toward private businesses, and the consequent changes in the opportunities available to them, brought about important changes in the position of the private sector in the economy and in Chinese politics. The 1980s witnessed dramatic growth both in the size of the private sector as a whole and in the size and impact of particular firms. At the same time the private economy became much more intimately connected with other ownership sectors, both through the increasing variety of relationships described in chapter 4, and through a complex variety of administrative arrangements, which stemmed from further attempts to reform state and collective enterprises and from the private sector's uncertain relationship with the state administration. This chapter discusses these developments in the role and nature of the private economy.

The Growing Size and Impact of the Private Sector

The registered private sector is still very small in proportion to the Chinese economy as a whole. The figures in Table 1.1 (page 6)

This chapter is based partly on Susan Young, "Policy, Practice and the Private Sector in China" and "Wealth But Not Security: Attitudes towards Private Business in China in the 1980s," both published in the *Australian Journal of Chinese Affairs*, no. 21 (January 1989), pp. 57–80, and no. 25 (January 1991), pp. 115–38, respectively. I am grateful to the editors for permission to reprint this material.

show extremely rapid growth in the number of registered individual businesses, but from very small beginnings, so that after a decade of reform policies there were still fewer than 15 million private businesses registered with the ICB. Although these businesses were making inroads into manufacturing, food processing, construction, transport, and other industries, private businesses were still predominantly involved in retailing, catering, and services, yet even in these trades they only made up less than a fifth of retail value in official statistics and scarcely showed at all in industrial output figures. The statistics recorded by the Ministry of Agriculture show that the private sector, even only the *recognized* private sector, became much more significant in the rural economy, making up over a quarter of gross industrial output value in township enterprises from 1989 onward, but the fact remains that, in relation to the national economy, the acknowledged private sector remains small.[1]

It is these official figures, especially the lower figures of the State Statistical Bureau and the ICB, on which official policy statements and discussions of the private sector in China have been based. However, as noted in chapter 1, private businesses are in fact much more significant than official statistics indicate. First, even the official figures, known to be far too low, show a remarkable impact for a small private sector that began virtually from scratch in 1978. The very rapidity of its growth was, in itself, a serious challenge to traditional assertions about the superiority of the socialist sectors. Second, the importance of the private sector in the rural economy was virtually ignored in official statements that the private sector remained a marginal "supplement" to the publicly owned economy. Third, while the overall share of private businesses in the national economy was not large, they did much better in particular localities and trades. For example, as early as 1984 sales by private restaurants in Changchun were ahead of state and collective restaurants by 13.5 million yuan and 9.47 million yuan respectively.[2] In the tailoring trade, private businesses produced two-thirds of Harbin's tailored clothes in 1983.[3] Private transporters were recorded as handling

9.9 percent of total goods transported in China in 1984, but in the first half of 1985 in Chengde, private and joint operators handled 2.4 million of the total 2.7 million tonnes of goods transported.[4] In many areas, private operators handled as much as one-third of passenger transport by 1988;[5] in Jiangxi it was calculated that privately run (although not necessarily privately *owned*) transport exceeded state and collective transport by 45 percent.[6] Chinese researchers' surveys also confirm that by the late 1980s the private sector was much larger than official statistics suggested, with estimates of the private share of gross output value ranging from 40 to 60 percent in some more developed regions.[7] In Changle county, Fujian, more than 95 percent of enterprises were privately owned (though not always registered as such) in 1988, and they made up 74.36 percent of the county's gross output value in 1987.[8]

New Opportunities for Private Entrepreneurs

As the 1980s progressed, the influence of private businesses was also enhanced by their formation of relationships with other ownership sectors and among themselves. With reforms to make state enterprises more independent and profit-oriented, the forms of ownership and management in the economy became more complex, and the simple trinity of state, collective, and individual began to be superseded. As Liu Guoguang put it in 1986, "Ownership by the whole people, collective ownership, and individual ownership, are no longer separate from one another, and there are no insurmountable barriers between various forms of ownership."[9] As discussed in chapter 4, while the small size and independence of most private businesses could be an advantage in terms of flexibility, their size and their lack of political clout could disadvantage them severely in competition with state and collective units for supplies, business premises, and so on. One way in which private businesses sometimes sought to overcome this was to club together in various cooperative formations, although this appears to have been rare. For example, a group of vegetable sellers might pool their funds to buy in bulk: a group of twenty-four stallholders who did this in Qiqiha'er in Heilongjiang managed to double their incomes.[10] Other groups of private businesspeople organized collectively to solve the problem of business premises by pooling their funds to build market buildings.[11]

Attachment to State and Collective Enterprises

More significant than collective action to solve business problems were the increasing links across ownership sectors. In addition to increasing business links as state and collective units bought the output or services of private businesses, an important factor was the ways in which private businesses sought to solve problems of prejudice and supply difficulties by attaching themselves to a state or collective unit. The practice of leasing counters in state-run shops to *getihu*, referred to in chapter 4, is one example of this: Chengdu's famous mosquito-net manufacturer, Yang Yi'an, moved into the Shanghai market via the Number One Department Store in December 1986 and proceeded to equal the store's previous year's sales of nets in six months.[12] Private operators leasing counters in state shops benefited not only from the better environment but also from the better public image of state shops, which, while not famous for their efficiency or good service, did have the reputation of being more honest than *getihu*. On another level, the leasing of counters to *getihu* was a significant acknowledgment of their economic strengths and was one aspect of the increasing integration of the private sector into the economic system.

Another form of cooperation between private businesses and state or collective units was the *guahu*, or "hanger-on," system. This is best known in Wenzhou but was also found elsewhere and was one of the most common methods of obtaining a false collective registration. In some cases the publicly owned unit and the private business genuinely cooperated: a private business manufacturing or marketing for a publicly owned unit used the unit's name or received other assistance such as supplies of raw materials. This could even amount to a takeover by a state unit in competition, with the private operator having no decision-making power and being similar to an employee paid piece-rates. In other cases, the private business merely paid the state unit a fee for the use of its name and used this name, and the collective license thus gained, to do business entirely on its own account.[13]

Such arrangements helped individuals overcome supply difficulties and avoid restrictions applied to private businesses and provided them with more security. In some cases the state unit benefited simply from its commission, but this could also be a cheap and easy way for a state unit to expand its operations, avoiding the costs that would normally be associated with buying its own equipment and providing facilities for workers. The Guangzhou Postal and Telecommunications Bureau, for example, used this method to expand its services, with arrangements in which individuals or collectives provided space and equipment, and the Bureau provided technical assistance and support.[14] The *guahu* system was also seen by authorities as a way of making administrative control easier, since it served to unite individual businesses under one umbrella organization. For example, the municipal government of Botou city in Hebei, when it began actively to support the growth of private businesses, made a point of encouraging this system for just this reason.[15] On the other hand, the large number of private businesses using this method to register as collectives makes it difficult to assess accurately the size of the private sector. Furthermore, as is clear from the above description, *guahu* arrangements were highly varied and often legally unclear. Yet under the encouragement given to state and collective enterprises to make their own efforts to earn profits, such arrangements proliferated. The State Council itself supported such relationships with its March 1986 regulations on promoting horizontal economic links, which specifically encouraged all kinds of contractual links across ownership lines.[16]

Opportunities in the Public Sector:
Leasing and Contracting

Parallel to the rapid growth and conspicuous success of the private sector were reforms aimed at improving the performance of state and collective enterprises, and these too provided opportunities for private entrepreneurs. Many of the reforms within the publicly owned sectors sought to obtain some of the perceived advantages of private ownership—enterprise autonomy, managerial responsibility, responsiveness to economic opportunities, and improved incentives—without forsaking China's commitment to public ownership. The example of household contracting in agriculture was therefore followed by experiments in contracting or leasing out the management of small and medium industrial and commercial enterprises.

The rationale for this was the idea of separating ownership rights from management rights (*liang quan fenli*), so that managers would be more personally responsible and more freely able to respond to market signals. This offered a way in which the management of enterprises could be radically altered without, in theory, affecting their ownership status at all. In rural collective enterprises contracting became very common, but varied in practice between a rather limited rearrangement of administrative procedures, to a process of progressive privatization of an enterprise. Contracting (*chengbao*) was supposed to differ from leasing (*zulin*) in the degree of control over management retained by the owners of the enterprise, but in many cases an individual would take over the full operation of the enterprise, with the collective simply collecting a percentage of profits or even a predetermined amount as rent.[17]

In state enterprises and the urban collective sector, such an arrangement would usually be spelled out in the form of enterprise leasing. The leasing of small state commercial enterprises began to spread in 1983 and was formalized in a State Council circular on the reform of the urban commercial system in July 1984.[18] The bulk of leased enterprises were in fact collectively owned, and in urban areas the majority have been small-scale commercial or service enterprises. By June 1987, however, twenty-seven thousand state-owned commercial enterprises had been leased out.[19] Leasing of medium-size enterprises in urban areas began in 1987, but this was controversial, and a 1987 article in the party journal *Red Flag* pronounced that leasing was "less suitable" for larger or industrial enterprises.[20] Leasing and contracting have both been confined mainly to unprofitable enterprises, although in the relatively open theoretical atmosphere of 1988, it was suggested that if leasing could save loss-making enterprises, surely it should be considered for profitable enterprises, too.[21]

Leasing or contracting out a state or collective enterprise was one way in which an individual could go into business, as it solved the problem of premises, lack of capital, and very often supply sources as well. Although leaseholders were supposed to guarantee the payment of the agreed rent and take responsibility for losses (and in contracted enterprises, often fulfill certain targets as well), many had no way of doing so but were allowed to lease anyway. In one study, the collateral of leaseholders and their guarantors generally had a real value of around 6,000 yuan, whereas the enterprises they were leasing had assets of 200,000 to 300,000 yuan.[22] Successful leaseholders could achieve high incomes, and this could be a good way of accumulating enough capital to start up independently.

Alternatively, leasing and contracting have often led to the partial or complete privatization of enterprise ownership, as operators have invested their profits in the enterprise in their own name. In a 1988 article, Liu Wenpu describes how in some places, such privatization of rural collective enterprises began in the early stages of rural reforms through experiments with the contract system. Liu gives the example of a bottletop factory established by a production team. When the factory proved unprofitable, it was "contracted" to an individual in 1981. The arrangement was really a straightforward lease, in which the individual agreed to pay 10 percent of the profits plus a set rent on equipment. The contractor then invested in the factory, so that by 1983, 81.5 percent of the capital belonged to him. With depreciation and the overall development of the factory, the collective assets were by this time so insignificant that he was able to hand them back to the collective and carry on running the factory as a private enterprise.[23] In a 1986 study of thirty leased or contracted enterprises in Shenyang, the contractors' own investment was generally 25 to 30 percent of the original fixed assets and climbing.[24] In the case of one Jiangsu township reported in 1993, the process had become formalized, with a specification in contracting agreements that both the collective and the contractors, who were each entitled to 50 percent of above-target profits, must then reinvest 50 percent of that in the enterprise. Many contracts specify a proportion of enterprise income to be invested in the enterprise, but this arrangement appears to require the investment *after* profits have become the property of the contractor.[25]

Discussions of leasing and contracting in the Chinese media tended to emphasize that the ownership of the enterprise did not change and therefore the dominance of public ownership would not be affected. But even without the change in asset shares described above, the handing over of an enterprise in return for rent raised important questions as to how public ownership should be manifested. Most of the issues were canvassed in the debate over the "Guan Guangmei phenomenon" conducted in the letters pages of *Jingji ribao* (Economic Daily) in June–July 1987. In 1985, Guan Guangmei had leased a grocery store in the Liaoning city of Benxi and promptly increased its annual profits by 40 percent. In 1986 she leased another two shops and in January 1987, with a partner, leased five more, forming a "leasing consortium" with one thousand employees, one-third of sales in the city's nonstaple food trade, and one-half of profits.[26] Guan made sweeping changes in the management of the shops, the most controversial of which involved working conditions and payment. Her own income was also a matter of concern, as she was legally entitled to the net profits of 42,000 yuan, although she did not in fact take this much as personal income.[27]

Jingji ribao opened the debate with a letter from Guan Guangmei herself, in which she complained that since leasing more shops she was encountering a lot of opposition from cadres who said that what she was doing was bourgeois liberalization and unsocialist. Guan denied this, basing her argument on the foundation of the reformist case, the supremacy of the productive forces. She had instituted a system of paying managers' wages according to profits, and staff wages according to sales:

> But this method is seen by some as a capitalist management method, as unequal and exploitative, as "reaping the fruits of others' labor." No matter how I look at it I can't understand: enterprises that in the past had declining profits or losses, and were even unable to pay out salaries, were socialist; now enterprises that have profits and give bonuses are capitalist. It's very strange![28]

This was the beginning of a six-week debate on whether leased enterprises were capitalist or socialist. Many correspondents were not convinced by Guan's argument that it was economic results that counted:

> We cannot say that since an enterprise's profits have increased, it has paid taxes to the state, and workers' incomes have increased, so it is a socialist enterprise; likewise, we cannot say that enterprises that run at a loss are therefore capitalist.[29]

Although *Jingji ribao* published letters expressing a wide range of opinions, the bulk of those chosen, as well as the editorials, came down in favor of leasing. In addition to emphasizing its economic benefits to the state, employees, and consumers, the writers attempted to counter the charges of capitalism. Leaseholders' high incomes were justified by their hard work, responsibility, and risk, and readers were reminded that only a small portion of enterprises were leased: the majority of state enterprises were still state-run and would preserve the socialist nature of the economy as a whole.[30]

Above all, it was argued that leasing was simply a reform of management, not of ownership: a separation of ownership and management rights. However, problems with this argument were clearly illustrated by the case of Guan Guangmei. These included the power held by leaseholders over employees, the leaseholders' autonomy in investment decisions, the ownership of new assets acquired after leasing, and the role of the party: questions that were fundamental to socialist politics. Guan Guangmei made a point of improving employees' economic and working conditions, offering increased wages and bonuses, and many benefits for her work force. However, these were accompanied by crushing fines (50 yuan in one example) for bad performance.[31] Guan also dramatically cut the number of managerial staff in her enterprises and herself acted as party secretary of the consortium.[32]

In view of this, many commentators questioned the significance of the state's continued ownership of enterprises, if management were really handed over. One letter in the Guan Guangmei debate stated:

> The reason why capitalists are able to exploit the workers is not only that they have the power of ownership, but more importantly that they have the power of use of the enterprise and the power of allocation of the results of labor. When enterprises are leased, these two powers go to the lessee. Under these conditions, to say that the enterprise is a socialist enterprise as before is hard to accept. If so, it is a devalued socialist enterprise.[33]

In fact Guan Guangmei had been allowed unusual freedom; many other reports suggest that leaseholders often do not have full management rights, particularly in the staffing and investment decisions that are of central importance to the lessors. To them, the enterprise's role in social welfare remains extremely important, and leaseholders have found it almost impossible to sack employees.[34]

The Rise of the *Siying Qiye*

While contracting and leasing provided one way for enterprising individuals to operate, if not legally own, enterprises of some size, others were developing such enterprises independently. Called *siying qiye* (privately run enterprises) to distinguish them from the smaller *getihu* (individual households), these enterprises were an important aspect of the growth of private business in China. At first, they were often called *siren qiye* (private personal enterprises), but this obviously sounded too capitalistic, and *siying qiye* came to be the official term. Such enterprises, defined as privately owned enterprises employing more than seven people, began to develop early in the reform program, but because of their politically sensitive nature were not regulated for until 1988. The *siying qiye* raised many questions as to the role of private enterprise in China and other socialist countries. Their size and impact posed a striking challenge to the old scenario of a small, restricted private sector of individual or family businesses, controlled and dominated by the socialist system. Indeed the background and evolution of these enterprises cast serious doubts on the ability of that system to exert control effectively in a reform environment. Their nature, and the type of person who ran them, suggested a closer integration of the private and public sectors and more scope for private entrepreneurs to exert political and economic influence. Finally, all these factors combined to make the *siying qiye* a difficult problem for policymakers and administrators that had not been adequately addressed.

As discussed in chapter 2, the argument used to suggest that private business would not be a danger to socialism was that the private sector would be restricted. Businesses would be kept small in size, leaving no scope for exploitation or the accumulation of capital. Such small businesses would remain marginal and dependent on the socialist publicly owned economy and, therefore, could not have much impact on the socialist nature of the economy as a whole. However as chapters 3 and 4 have shown, the impact of reforms on the state sector changed this situation, making the public economy less amenable as a tool for limiting private business. At the same time, pressures on administrators to develop their local economies, and to provide employment, continued to combine with limited state resources to encourage recourse to alternative means of development, among them the private economy. As a result of these pressures, *getihu* who wanted to take on more employees, or other private investors with capital waiting to be used, found that the rules designed to prevent the development of capitalist enterprise could often be broken or bent.

Because private businesses were owned by individuals who employed others and profited from their labor, the question of how many people they might employ was a much more sensitive issue than other factors of size. Individual businesses, for years the only type of domestic privately owned business acknowledged by the government, were limited to seven employees. This limit was retained even in 1983, when many other restrictions on individual businesses were removed, and the number of employees remained the sole criterion by which *getihu* and *siying qiye* were differentiated in the 1980s. But the same logic that worked against the limitation of individual businesses' assets and technological level applied here, too, particularly as the type of enterprise and level of development of most private businesses made increasing labor inputs an obvious method of expansion. In addition, there was the pressure of the unemployment problem: one of the major reasons for promoting the individual economy was to provide jobs. If a private watch-repairer who took on three apprentices was doing the state a favor, did not the same apply to the baker who employed a hundred handicapped youths?[35]

Individuals who wished to employ more than seven people were not slow to play on these points. Jiang Wei, a private businessman who set up a joint venture with a Hong Kong company, when invited to speak to the students of Liaoning University, pointed out that promoting private enterprise provided jobs for thousands of young people.[36] A report on Wenzhou building machinery manufacturer Liu Shangtan, whose 1986 output was worth 1 million yuan, emphasized his role as an employer. It quoted him as saying he would not quit while the going was good (as many entrepreneurs did, for fear of a policy change) because if he did, what would become of the enterprise's 123 workers?[37]

It was the authorities promoting private business, as much as the entrepreneurs themselves, who wished to make this point; the case of Nian Guangjiu, the man behind Shazi Guazi melon seeds, is a good example. When Nian came under attack for tax evasion, exploitation, and poor treatment of employees, he was reported to have written to the Anhui party secretary in his own defense. His letter, published in full with the secretary's reply, pointed out that the Shazi Guazi Company provided a market for about five thousand melon seed growers and jobs not only for its own employees but also for independent retailers of Shazi Guazi. Furthermore, it would mend its ways and pay some 2 million yuan in taxes that year.[38] Whether Nian really wrote the letter as published hardly mattered: the point of its publication was to send a clear message of support for the private sector, based on economic motives. In fact, by the time the letter appeared in 1985, Nian's company had been taken over by two local-government companies, with Nian as manager, but the letter was printed as part of the campaign to promote private business anyway.[39]

Evolution of Policy toward Siying Qiye

Larger private enterprises began to appear as early as 1981, but at that time it was politically impossible for the party leadership to acknowledge and legitimize them: the debate on whether the small and ostensibly limited *getihu* were acceptable under socialism was only just getting into the open, and the reformists' arguments were predicated on the assertion that *getihu* would not be allowed to get any bigger. It is clear from the early growth of larger private enterprises that some leaders saw them as a logical and beneficial extension of the individual economy, but they could hardly have had this proclaimed as party policy in 1981. Instead, a policy of cautious and unpublicized experimentation was adopted, which put the development of larger private enterprises in local government hands.

The version of events related in interviews with officials and academics is that when *siying qiye* first began to appear, the Central Committee adopted a "wait and see" policy: that is, *siying qiye* would be allowed to develop, while the central government and public debate continued to ignore and even deny their existence. The real effect of central policies at this time, however, was explicitly to hand discretion over private enterprise development to local governments, while in many cases giving them strong incentives to exceed regulation limits. As mentioned in chapter 3, after 1984 statistical assessments of township enterprises, and the quotas for their development, began to list individual and joint enterprises. Central Committee Document No. 1 of that year acknowledged the usefulness of larger private enterprises to the reforms, and bent over backward to see their good side:

> Of enterprises that are currently exceeding regulation employment numbers, some have implemented systems different from *siren qiye*, for example, taking a certain proportion of after-tax profits to be invested in collective assets; regulating the limits of dividends and owners' income; issuing a certain amount of profit to workers, etc. These thus have elements of cooperative economy to varying degrees. We should help them continue to improve, and they may be treated differently from capitalist employers.[40]

When even limiting the amount of profits to be taken as income (the remainder no doubt reinvested and still privately owned) is interpreted as a step toward cooperativization, it is not hard to see how almost any private enterprise could avoid being seen as a "capitalist employer." This gave tacit approval to the registration of private enterprises as collectives, which allowed them to minimize political opprobrium and risk, and benefit from the range of discriminatory policies aimed precisely at maintaining the dominance of the publicly owned economy.

Through the mid-1980s, large private enterprises were not really illegal, they were merely unregulated. It is true that there was no place for them in the constitution, but on the other hand there were no laws or regulations *against* them. Regulations said that *getihu* could not exceed seven employees. But in practice that merely meant that once they did, they could no longer properly be considered *getihu*. There were regulations for cooperative enterprises, for specialized households, for collective enterprises. Each of these regulations specified how an enterprise conforming to a certain definition should be run. But Chinese economic regulations were not so proscriptive as to deny the possibility of other types of enterprise developing: that was left to be decided by party policy. And so, when faced with policies directing them to develop their local economies, to expand the role of the market, to increase employment and raise incomes, and to promote a variety of ownership types, administrators in both state organs and local governments did not try to ban large private enterprises, but to find a place for them in the smorgasbord of regulations and administrative procedures at their disposal.

Large private enterprises developed in different ways: some were *getihu* that grew larger and took on more employees; some derived from the leasing of state or collective enterprises to individuals; or they could be established by joint investors. Since until June 1988 there was no official category of registration as a *siying qiye*, administrative organs dealt with such enterprises in various ways. Some of the smaller ones were registered as *getihu*, but given permission to employ more than seven people. This appears to have been more common in urban areas. In rural areas, it was much more common for larger private enterprises to obtain at least partial inclusion in the collective category by one means or another.

One way of doing this was to view *zhuanyehu* (rural specialized households) and *lianhu* (joint enterprises) as part of the collective economy, but vary their treatment on specific matters. Not all *zhuanyehu* were run by peasants who specialized: for example, a man I interviewed in 1988 had left his job at a Chengdu dairy company to move out to the rural outskirts of Chengdu, rent land, and build a modern chicken farm. With the legalization of large private enterprises in 1988, however, he was under pressure to obtain a *siying qiye* license. Likewise, many *lianhu* interviewed simply had a relative as a sleeping partner.

It was also very common for private enterprises to obtain a collective license by paying an "administration fee" to a state or collective unit or local government organization such as a street committee or township business corporation, in order to get its stamp on their application. During the 1980s the fee was generally 1–2 percent of output value or 5–10 percent of turnover. (One private entrepreneur I interviewed in Chengdu had done very well for himself: the unit he approached had little confidence in his venture and demanded a fixed annual fee of a few hundred yuan instead of the 1 percent of gross output value that he suggested. As his factory's output value was 300,000 yuan in 1987 and a projected 600,000 yuan in 1988, this proved to be a good thing for him.) Alternatively, some entrepreneurs managed to get collective licenses by claiming to be collectives in their own right, without an umbrella unit. This was done by arrangements such as those described in the quotation above from Document No. 1 of 1984. The director of one company I visited in Xindu county on the outskirts of Chengdu, who had started a five-factory concern in 1982, found it expedient in 1983 to turn over a portion of the assets as shares to staff members. This portion remained no more than 10 percent and the director retained total control of the enterprise, yet he was thus able to claim that his was a "collective share company." The owner of a large fashion retail and manufacturing company in Chengdu, interviewed in 1988, distributed a certain part of the profits to staff as bonuses: hence her company was "collective" even though she was a leading member of the local Individual Laborers' Association. This woman made a point of maintaining an excellent relationship with cadres who could influence her enterprise, and neither she nor they seemed to find the apparent contradiction difficult to live with at that time.

The collective registration of private enterprises was often encouraged by local cadres who wanted to fill quotas for promoting local industry and commerce and therefore were willing to give collective registration to private enterprises that exceeded the employment limits for *getihu*, in order to utilize their investment. In Anhui, for example, many private enterprises developed in this way after 1984, when the provincial government initiated a drive to promote township enterprises.[41] The growth of larger private enterprises was often an integral part of the economic development of a community and could be achieved only by close cooperation between private entrepreneurs and local government.[42] But the informality, even illegality, of such arrangements also gave local authorities great leverage over private enterprises, which they used to ensure that these enterprises made considerable contributions to the welfare either of corrupt cadres, or of their communities.

In many places, the relationship between large and small private businesses and local officials was quite different. Smaller ones were often left largely to themselves except for the collection of fees, but larger enterprises, because of their more complex needs and their impact on the community, tended to have a much closer relationship with local authorities. Very few enterprises were able to grow to any significant size without justifying their existence by making clear contributions to the community. Through direct pressure from cadres, public opinion, or both, entrepreneurs would be prevailed upon to donate large sums to local projects (successful entrepreneurs have funded whole schools and tree-planting programs), provide jobs or free goods and services to members of poor families, and train apprentices so that others too might learn the secret of how to become rich.[43]

Much has been made in the Chinese press of personal graft on the part of cadres. Although this did occur, there was also a consistent tendency to make private entrepreneurs contribute to the whole community. Of course, private entrepreneurs still retained most of the profits for themselves, but in many cases the effect of such pressures was that, while they were not formally obliged to hand over 10 or 15 percent of profits, as would a "real" collective enterprise, their actual contribution could be of a similar scale.[44] Sometimes private entrepreneurs who obtained collective registration were in fact required to live up to it by handing over a percentage of profits. Some even found themselves forced to hand over the whole enterprise when the township decided to claim real ownership.[45]

One consequence of such arrangements was that private enterprises did remain constrained by the socialist system; but that system itself was an entity of many levels and conflicting interests, and by the late 1980s a tug-of-war developed between central and local governments over the control of the growing private sector. Belatedly, Central Committee Document No. 5 of 1987 formally acknowledged the role of the *siying qiye* and adopted a new policy toward them of "Allow to exist, improve administration, promote the good and limit the bad, and gradually guide" (*Yunxu cunzai, jiaqiang guanli, xingli yibi, zhubu yindao*).[46] The policy of gradual guidance was a continuation of the ideas expressed in 1984, that the larger private enterprises should be guided toward some form of cooperative or collective operation. Those who believed large-scale private employers to be incompatible with socialist goals felt that this should be quite a short process of encouraging oversized private enterprises to collectivize. The ICB's 1983 regulations on the registration of urban cooperatives and individual businesses had stated categorically that individual businesses should be changed into cooperatives once they passed regulation size.[47] But others were anxious to avoid a repetition of the socialist transformation of the 1950s and said that collectivization should be strictly voluntary.[48] The theory of the initial stage of socialism, expounded in Zhao Ziyang's report to the Thirteenth Party Congress in 1987, finally gave official recognition to the large private enterprises, the *siying qiye*, as a legitimate economic type, separate from individual businesses, and the projected time-span for this initial stage into the middle of the next century apparently meant that such "capitalistic" enterprises would be acceptable for a long time to come.[49]

By late 1987 the emphasis had turned to improved administration as the means by which state control over the private sector could be effected. This stance was confirmed in 1988, when ICB branches in some cities began to develop procedures for the registration and administration of *siying qiye*. Then in June 1988 the State Council passed a set of provisional regulations on *siying qiye*, accompanied by regulations on income tax on private enterprises and on personal income from private enterprises, to take effect on 1 July.[50] These regulations stated that *siying qiye*, defined as enterprises with privately owned assets and employing more than eight people, were a "supplement to the socialist publicly owned economy" and enjoyed the protection of the state. *Siying qiye* were divided into those owned by an individual investor, by partnerships of two or more people—the owners of both types retaining liability for the enterprise—and limited liability companies owned by between two and thirty shareholders. Special permission could also be given for enterprises of more than thirty shareholders, but *siying qiye* were not allowed to issue shares to the public. The regulations also dealt with employment and working conditions within private enterprises, including the stipulation that private enterprise labor contracts should be filed with the local labor bureau and that labor disputes should be handled according to the regulations for dealing with such disputes in state enterprises.

The Size and Impact of the Siying Qiye

Not surprisingly, in view of the variations described above, the exact number of these enterprises is difficult to determine. Local administrative organs and research institutions have published their own surveys and reports, but have had different ideas as to where to draw the line between a *getihu* and a *siying qiye*. The state ICB, and presumably its local branches, has stuck to its regulations and called any enterprise that admits to being privately owned, and employs eight or more people, a *siying qiye*. Until 1988, its statistics, of necessity, counted only those enterprises that had been registered as *getihu*, yet were in fact larger than *getihu* size. A 1986 study of Shanghai's private sector argued that the line should vary from place to place and trade to trade; for their own purposes the authors chose a cut-off point of ten employees.[51] The policy research office of the Wenzhou municipal committee was, not surprisingly, more liberal, and considered thirty employees an appropriate number.[52] Some surveys include enterprises that are in fact private, but registered as collective; others do not. Euphemistically labeling these enterprises "privately run" also causes problems, as some surveys take the term literally and include any enterprises that are run (for example, leased) by individuals.

Estimates as to the number of *siying qiye* nationwide varied in late 1987 and 1988 between two and three hundred thousand. At that time the only figure the ICB released was that of the 115,000 individual enterprises registered as having eight or more employees.[53] In June 1988 Ren Zhonglin, director of the state ICB, announced that China had 225,000 *siying qiye* employing 3.6 million people and making up 1 percent of gross value of industrial output.[54] This figure included some enterprises registered as collectives, but was probably still much too low. It was difficult for the ICB to determine how many "collective" enterprises were in fact private, and many did not really come under its jurisdiction. One survey suggested that 0.8 percent of rural households were *siying qiye* in 1985, which on official figures would give a total of 1.53 million.[55] A survey of twenty thousand rural households found that 0.74 percent were employers, and based on this survey one Chinese estimate put the total number of *siying qiye* at around one million in 1988.[56] Since 1989 the ICB has published figures on registered *siying qiye* (see Table 1.1, page 6), but these remain much lower than the real number of enterprises that are privately owned and run. An academic in Sichuan estimated that 8–12 million employees worked in *siying qiye* in early 1990.[57]

Local figures also imply a large number of these enterprises. Hebei's Handan area claimed nearly twenty-two thousand *siying qiye* of various kinds—including joint stock companies and partnerships—responsible for 22 percent of total output value.[58] Figures on the individual economy in Beijing show a ratio of 295 businesses to 295 personnel in 1978; by the end of 1986 it was 9,174 businesses to 142,000 personnel: an average of 15 people per business.[59] In certain areas *siying qiye* have come to play a major role in the economy. According to one report, around 50 percent of Wenzhou's revenue in 1987 was derived from private business, 32 percent of it from *siying qiye*.[60] In Wuchuan county, Guangdong, *siying qiye* with more than eleven employees made up approximately 43 percent of gross industrial and agricultural output value in 1987, and 44 percent of revenue.[61]

In spite of occasional well-publicized cases of extremely large private enterprises with millionaire owners, the bulk of *siying qiye* remained relatively small. The ICB estimated in 1988 that 70–80 percent of *siying qiye* had fewer than thirty employees, with less than 1 percent employing more than one hundred; the average overall was sixteen employees per enterprise. The average capital of *siying qiye* was estimated to be 50,000 yuan.[62] In Anhui in 1987, 40 percent of *siying qiye* employed more than twenty people, had assets exceeding 100,000 yuan, and output value exceeding 200,000 yuan. Over 10 percent had an output value of over 500,000 yuan.[63] Sources of capital tended to be the same for *siying qiye* as for *getihu* (not surprisingly since many began as *getihu*), except that increasing size gave *siying qiye* more scope for borrowing from financial institutions, as they were more likely to have the collateral and connections necessary for such loans. A common source of extra funds for larger enterprises, especially in rural areas, was the practice of requiring new employees to invest a sum of money, usually a few hundred yuan but sometimes more, in the enterprise. This practice is also common to rural collective enterprises and indicates the high demand for jobs in rural industry, as well as the shortage of capital.[64]

Many of the examples of large private enterprises in published accounts have grown up from individual businesses, and are in light manufacturing (e.g., clothes, mosquito nets, cassette head cleaner) or catering and food processing (e.g., bakeries, ice blocks, melon seeds). However, these types of *siying qiye* are probably prevalent in newspaper reports because they are conveniently located in cities, rather than because they are typical of *siying qiye*. Despite an inevitable overlap, there is a distinct difference both in fields of activity and in location between the majority of small individual businesses and the majority of the larger *siying qiye*. Because of these differences, the growth and acceptance of the *siying qiye* marked a new phase in the development of private enterprise in China.

Besides being bigger and therefore able to have a more obvious effect on the economy, *siying qiye* tend to be engaged in industry, mining, transport, and construction, with a smaller though still significant proportion in consumer industries. According to one source, 82 percent of *siying qiye*, 87 percent of their personnel, and 83 percent of their capital were to be found in industry, transport, and construction in 1988.[65] This is significant for the status and security of private business as a whole in China. Productive enterprises are more prestigious and more politically acceptable, getting away from the notion, found both in Confucian Chinese tradition and in Marxism, of the merchant who merely buys and sells, extracting an exploitative income in the process. The growth in scale and the wider range of trades also means that the private sector is becoming more integrated with the rest of the Chinese economy, as the customers of these enterprises are state enterprises and local government organs, as well as individual consumers. Like smaller businesses, larger firms form direct links with state enterprises, as for example a workshop of sixty people making bulbs for electronic watches for the Shenyang Electronic Instrument Factory for overseas sale.[66]

Private enterprises with overseas links appeared quite early. For example, the Liaoning entrepreneur Jiang Wei set up a joint venture with a Hong Kong firm dealing in photo-processing and photocopying in 1985,[67] and a Tianjin maker of hot water heaters upgraded his product to export quality with a Japanese design and entered a joint venture with a U.S. company in 1984.[68] Many Chinese entrepreneurs have set up export processing enterprises, particularly in Guangdong, and this began much earlier than was officially acknowledged. For example, in Dongwan county after

1984, private investors were encouraged by local authorities to register their enterprises as "collectives" so that they could do export processing and compensation trade, at that time forbidden to private enterprises. By 1987 these private enterprises accounted for over 15 percent of the area's foreign processing and joint venture business.[69]

Throughout the 1980s, most *siying qiye* developed in rural areas. This probably reflected a greater degree of economic freedom in rural areas and more flexible attitudes to administrative problems such as registration as a *zhuanyehu*, or collective enterprise, as well as much easier logistics with regard to space and supplies. Premises of the size needed for even a small factory are extremely difficult to obtain in the cities, especially for an individual, and some city planning authorities have had a policy of discouraging industrial development in the already crowded and polluted urban areas. As China's reforms continued, however, *siying qiye* naturally took advantage of the new urban markets for construction, building interiors, entertainment, and services of various kinds, resulting in a switch to an urban majority in the registration figures. Some of this change probably results from more precise registration and more effective ICB administration in urban areas. The recent growth in urban *siying qiye* is certainly real, but it is doubtful whether they really outnumber their rural counterparts.

An important factor in the nature of rural *siying qiye* is the type of people involved in running them. Here there is a marked difference from small *getihu*: according to one report, 60 percent of owners of *siying qiye* in rural areas were originally management or supply and marketing staff in state or collective enterprises or cadres in production teams or brigades.[70] Another survey gave the figure as around 46 percent.[71] Still other officials and personnel on key units such as state supply bureaus are often involved less directly, with positions as consultants, directors, or by having relatives employed in the enterprise. In Wenzhou, famous for the development of its private sector, 70 percent of cadres at township level were found to receive benefits from relatives in private enterprise.[72] Entrepreneurs with a cadre or management background are the people most likely to have the knowledge and management skills to run a larger enterprise successfully. It is also they who have the contacts that enable them to lease land, obtain electricity or fuel and raw materials, to smooth the path of leasing procedures, and so on. There are two sides to this question. Some private entrepreneurs complain that they are forced to give jobs or directorships to cadres and their relatives when they have no wish to do so. On the other hand, some entrepreneurs seek this close involvement with cadres and other useful and influential people to make doing business both easier and more secure. This close relationship between private enterprises and rural authorities, both in their personnel and in the administrative arrangements described earlier, means that rural private enterprises are often not able to be entirely "private" in their operation, but it also means they are firmly entrenched within the rural economy.

Conclusion

The growing influence of the private sector, complex and varied relationships between private enterprise and other sectors, and the tremendous growth in the size of both the private sector as a whole and private enterprises themselves, meant that the original concept of a marginal sector of small individual businesses became outdated. The growth and eventual acknowledgment of the *siying qiye* is of particular significance, indicating a much firmer foothold for private enterprise in the Chinese economy. The original idea that private businesses would be constrained by their dependence on the state sector was never very workable and became steadily less so as reforms to make state enterprises more independent and profit-seeking took effect. This posed new problems of policy and administration, as alternative methods of administrative and legal regulation needed to be developed and implemented. Here, however, the downside of the bottom-up implementation of the reforms began to manifest itself: by the time the central government sought to claw back some control over enterprise development, local governments, and administrators at the lower levels of the various state bureaucracies, had established a range of informal interests that they were loath to give up.

Notes

1. *ZXQN*, 1993, p. 147.
2. Li Bin and Zhao Ming, "Geti jingji zuoyong de bianhua," p. 51.
3. *Ha'erbin ribao*, 12 November 1983, p. 2.
4. *JJRB*, 17 August 1985, p. 2; *RMRB*, 14 September 1985, p. 2.
5. Yan Ying'an, "Dui geti keyun jiage yao jiaqiang guanli," p. 51.
6. *ZGGSB*, 20 March 1989, p. 1.
7. See Zhang Kai, "The Development of Private Enterprises in China."
8. Chen Jianhua, "Cong wu xu dao you xu," p. 42.
9. Liu Guoguang, "Guanyu suoyouzhi guanxi gaige de ruogan wenti."
10. *JJCK*, 18 January 1988, p. 1.
11. For example, *RMRB*, 10 September 1985, p. 2.
12. *RMRB*, 14 December 1986, p. 1, and 25 August 1987, p. 2.
13. *JJRB*, 26 November 1987, p. 2; Huang Jiajing, "Wenzhou de guahu jingying ji qi wanshan wenti."
14. *JJCK*, 2 January 1988, p. 1.
15. *Zhongguo xiangzhen qiye bao* (China Township Enterprise News), 28 March 1988, p. 1.
16. "Guowuyuan guanyu jinyibu tuidong hengxiang jingji lianhe ruogan wenti de guiding" (State Council decision on some questions in further promoting horizontal economic links), 23 March 1986, in Falu chubanshe fagui bianjibu, eds., *Siying qiye changyong falü shouce*, pp. 312–20.
17. Zhongguo shehui kexueyuan nongcun fazhan yanjiusuo siying jingji yanjiuzu, "Wei siying qiye wending, fazhan chuangzao lianghao de shehui jingji huanjing."
18. *Beijing Review*, no. 35 (27 August 1984), p. 4; *JJRB*, 1 August 1984, p. 1.
19. *RMRB*, 7 March 1988, p. 5. For reports on leased state enterprises see *RMRB*, 25 April 1984, p. 2; 26 August 1984, p. 2; *JJRB*, 5 July 1984, p. 1; *Zhongguo shangye bao* (Chinese Commerce), 10 November 1987, p. 2; Peng Heming, "Yixiang zushi qiye biange de zhongda cuoshi."
20. Zheng Li, Liu Zhaonian, and Xiao Wentong, "Zulin jingying de butong xingshi."
21. *JJRB*, 6 March 1988, p. 1. For reports of successful economic results from leasing, see *JJRB*, 21 February 1987, p. 1; and *RMRB*, 19 June 1987, p. 2.
22. Guo Yongjie, "Zulinzhi de bibing ji duice." See also the comment on this article in *Jingji yu guanli yanjiu* (Studies in Economics and Management),

no. 3, 1987; and Hunan sheng Anhua xianwei bangongshi diaoyan shi, "Dui zulin jingying zhong jige wenti de tantao," p. 27.

23. Liu Wenpu, "Lun nongcun jiti qiye siyinghua wenti."

24. He and Zhu, "Geti jingji de fazhan."

25. *Zhongguo xiangzhen qiye bao*, 20 October 1993, p. 3.

26. *JJRB*, 13 June 1987, p. 1. See also Benxi shi tigai ban, "Cong zulin yige shangdian fazhan wei shangye zulin jituan."

27. *JJRB*, 15 June 1987, p. 1.

28. *JJRB*, 12 June 1987, p. 1.

29. *JJRB*, 3 July 1987, p. 1.

30. For example, *JJRB*, 14 July 1987, p. 1; 18 July 1987, p. 1.

31. *JJRB*, 13 June 1987, p. 1.

32. *JJRB*, 12 June 1987, p. 1; figures on staff cuts in Benxi shi tigai ban, "Cong zulin yige shangdian," p. 277.

33. *JJRB*, 3 July 1987, p. 1.

34. Yang Zhaoxi and Liu Junying, "Zulin shi Beijing xiao shangye mianmao yi xin"; *JJCK*, 27 April 1988, p. 4; *JJCK*, 3 May 1988, p. 4.

35. *JJRB*, 12 November 1987, p. 2.

36. *RMRB*, 31 December 1985, p. 1.

37. *NMRB*, 10 August 1987, p. 1.

38. *GMRB*, 1 April 1984. For an English account of Nian's rise to fame, see Linda Hershkovitz, "The Fruits of Ambivalence," pp. 430–39.

39. See *RMRB*, 28 November 1987, p. 2. Apparently the now collectively owned Shazi Guazi company was not a success: this article details its failure with debts of over 900,000 yuan. Nian himself got into trouble again in 1989, when he was investigated on corruption and other charges and sentenced to three years in prison, eventually to be released early, according to a Hong Kong newspaper, after being favorably mentioned in Deng Xiaoping's southern tour speeches in 1992. See *SWB*, 9 April 1992, FE/1351 B2/5.

40. "Zhonggong zhongyang guanyu yi jiu ba si nian nongcun gongzuo de tongzhi" (Notice of the Central Committee concerning rural work in 1984), 1 January 1984, in Guojia xingzheng guanli ju geti jingji si and *Beijing ribao lilun bu*, eds., *Geti laodongzhe shouce*, p. 190.

41. *Zhongguo xiangzhen qiye bao*, 4 April 1988, p. 1.

42. The studies in Byrd and Lin, *China's Rural Industry*, also discuss this aspect in some detail.

43. See Odgaard, "Collective Control," and Oi, "Fate of the Collective." The degree of collective control implied in collective registration varies widely from place to place and even enterprise to enterprise. Oi has found in her fieldwork in Shandong that local governments demanded quite close involvement in management decisions in return for collective registration, while in Sichuan I have found many cases where enterprises were obliged to make financial contributions but were otherwise left to themselves. Community pressure on larger private enterprises also appears to be typical of rural areas rather than cities. Examples of such pressure in the literature tend to be rural, and both I and other researchers have found numerous urban private enterprises

that, apart from financial contributions required of enterprises of all owner-ships, were left largely alone.

44. *NMRB*, 16 December 1988, p. 2; Hu, Liu, and Chen, *Duo sediao de Zhongguo geti jingyingzhe*; He Wenfu, "Siying qiye."

45. Odgaard, "Collective Control"; *JJCK*, 9 December 1990 p. 1; 16 December 1990, p. 4.

46. Quoted in Ren Zhonglin, "Guanyu geti jingji wenti," p. 23; see also *JJRB*, 21 March 1987, p. 3.

47. Guojia gongshang xingzheng guanli ju, "Guanyu chengzhen hezuo jingying zuzhi he geti gongshangye hu zai dengji guanli zhong ruogan wenti de guiding" (Regulations on some questions in the registration of urban coop-eratively managed organizations and individual industrial and commercial households), quoted in Guojia gongshang xingzheng guanli ju geti si and *Beijing ribao* lilun bu, eds., *Geti laodongzhe shouce*, pp. 10–13.

48. For example, Wu Shangli, "Wo guo geti jingji falü diwei de tantao," p. 78.

49. Zhao Ziyang, "Yanzhe you Zhongguo tese de shehuizhuyi daolu qianjin," p. 2.

50. "Zhonghua renmin gongheguo siying qiye zanxing tiaoli" (People's Republic of China provisional regulations on private enterprises); "Zhonghua renmin gongheguo siying qiye suode shui zanxing tiaoli" (People's Republic of China provisional regulations on private enterprise income tax); and "Guowuyuan guanyu zhengshou siying qiye touzizhe geren shouru tiaojie shui de guiding" (Decision of the State Council on the collection of regulatory personal income tax from investors in private enterprises), 3 June 1988, in *RMRB*, 29 June 1988.

51. Chen Baorong and Chen Xiumei, "Shanghai siren jingji ruogan wenti tantao."

52. Tao Youzhi, "Luelun geti jingji," pp. 22–24.

53. *GMRB*, 16 March 1988, p. 1.

54. *RMRB*, 24 June 1988, p. 1.

55. He and Zhu, "Geti jingji de fazhan," p. 5.

56. Zhang Houyi and Qin Shaoxiang, "Siying jingji zai dangdai Zhongguo de shijian."

57. Ole Odgaard, personal communication.

58. *JJCK*, 5 November 1987, p. 1.

59. Li Jiali, "Geti gongshangye lingdao guanli tizhi jidai gaishan," p. 42.

60. *RMRB*, 4 April 1988, p. 1; *JJCK*, 14 November 1988, p. 4.

61. *JJCK*, 14 November 1987, p. 4.

62. *GMRB*, 16 March 1988, p. 1; Zhang and Qin, "Siying jingji," p. 4; *SWB*, 20 July 1988, FE/W0035 A/2.

63. *Zhongguo xiangzhen qiye bao*, 4 April 1988, p. 1.

64. For a description of employees bringing in funds in rural collective enterprises, see Oi, "Fate of the Collective."

65. Zhang and Qin, "Siying jingji," p. 4. Zhang and Qin include some enterprises registered as collectives in their figure. The ICB's statistics for

1990 (Guojia gongshang xingzheng guanli ju xinxi zhongxin, eds., *Zhongguo gongshang xingzheng tongji sishi nian*, pp. 154–56) give 68.6 percent of registered *siying qiye* in industry, 3.2 percent in construction, 1.3 percent in transport, and 19.7 percent in commerce, showing a slight increase in the commercial proportion over 1989. Many industrial private enterprises, however, are in rural areas and have found it easier to obtain collective registration.

66. *JJCK*, 18 December 1987, p. 1.

67. *JJRB*, 18 April 1985; *RMRB*, 31 December 1985; Li Yong and Chen Hongjun, "Geti jingji zai shewai jingji guanxi zhong falü diwei chutan."

68. *RMRB*, 31 October 1984, p. 2.

69. *RMRB*, 5 July 1988, p. 2; Pan Zuodi and Xie Jianmin, "Guanyu siren qiye ruogan wenti de tantao."

70. *RMRB*, 16 March 1988, p. 1.

71. Zheng Xinmiao, Wang Tongxin, and Wu Changling, "Dui nongcun siying jingji fazhan de lilun sikao ji zhengce jianyi," p. 48.

72. Ji and Zhu, "Siying qiye lirun," p. 49.

6

The Private Sector and State Control

The early proposals for developing private business maintained that it would remain marginal and be easily controlled because "in the scope of management, the supply of raw materials, price and taxation, it is subject to control and restriction by the public economy and by the state organs concerned."[1] In the 1980s, however, both "the public economy" and "the state organs concerned" became increasingly less reliable as arms of the central government. This was intentional, one of the fundamental reasons for the success of the reforms in promoting rapid growth, but it also came to be seen as a problem as China moved from an overregulated planned economy to a market economy in which existing regulation mechanisms were often inappropriate or ineffective, and appropriate replacements had yet to be developed. As the reforms developed, local administrators adapted to the new conditions to grasp a great deal of control over the local business scene, and in fact used established, pre-reform powers to make the most of the new opportunities offered under the reforms. They often enabled private business to develop, but they became proprietorial toward it, using it as a source of local income and power.

The preceding chapters have shown how, as a result of the widening opportunities generated by reform policies, many of the original logistical and administrative constraints on the private sector gave way. However, apart from legitimate market transactions and the policies aimed specifically at developing the private sector, the solutions that developed from the reform process were often informal ones, outside the regular channels of administrative control. They relied not on regulated, open procedures, but on personal connections, bribery, and go-betweens. Even those who operated more or less legitimately were usually well ahead of official policies and regulations, relying on ad hoc understandings with local administrators. The private sector was, of course, not the only stimulant of this informal economy; it had existed before the reforms, and unofficial dealings of government ministries and departments, publicly owned enterprises, and corrupt cadres became a major political issue in the second half of the 1980s. But the results of such dealings were particularly visible in the private sector, and its enforced "legal degeneracy" (to use Anders Åslund's term)[2] had significant implications for the nature of its development and its relationship with the state.

For the central government, reformists and conservatives alike, this course of development was a problem because it sabotaged the state's ability to control the economy effectively. False registrations made it impossible to collect reliable statistics on which to base economic policies; goods were diverted from planned distribution to be sold on the market, while the risks and costs associated with such diversion meant that markets for many goods were distorted by the high costs of corruption. In addition, much of the real administrative control over the private sector was vested in officials at the local level. Particularly in rural areas, it was they who developed the range of locally varied procedures for dealing with private businesses, and it was they who were left with the most power to extract revenue from this fast-growing and profitable sector. This was likely to make them proprietorial toward private enterprise—defending it from the demands of the central government while seeking to exploit it for local or personal ends—and more sympathetic to the interests of private entrepreneurs.[3]

The contradictory pressures arising from the attempt to place the structures of command economics alongside free market forces thus produced a middle stratum of "gatekeepers" whose control over goods, funds, or administrative approvals gave them considerable power over the course of economic development. Their interest lies not in further reform but in the maintenance of the disorderly, experimental transitional stage that gives the greatest degree of local or personal discretion. Local governments have used the freedoms given to them by the reforms to promote local economic growth, but this has made them less amenable to a revival of central economic control. Departmentalism is also a problem, as ministries and administrative departments have sought to promote economic activity that will increase their own sphere of influence. The private sector, because of its experimental status, has been in effect a kind of frontier territory, open to whichever organization can stake a claim.[4] While local authorities have responded to reform pressures by enabling the private sector to develop, and will fight to preserve it where possible, they do so in a way that maintains their own power over it and influences the way it develops.

Thus private sector development has been shaped by two major tensions—between old approaches to economic administration and the needs of a more modern market economy, and between central and local levels of administration—which are also major issues in the reform process as a whole. This chapter examines how these tensions have been manifested in two major issues in private sector administration: the policing and control of the private sector and taxation.

Private Business and the Bureaucracy: The ICB

The relationship of the private sector with the ICB clearly illustrates the above-mentioned tensions at work. One of the ICB's main tasks has been to try to maintain some degree of order and legality in the market and to enforce central regulations. On the other hand, the ICB was created to supervise market activity in the economy, and its own importance and influence, at all levels of government, grows in direct proportion to the growth of such activity.[5] The ICB has been right behind reforms that divert steadily more activity to the market (its own sphere of jurisdiction), away from the plan (controlled by the various ministries). As market reforms became more entrenched, the ICB became increasingly entrepreneurial, actively promoting and investing in market growth rather than merely policing it. In many of its activities to develop the private sector, such as the organization and building of markets in which private, collective, and state enterprises could all rent space, the ICB was indeed implementing policy, but it was also engaging in a little empire building.

Even though the ICB is a centrally led bureaucracy, the tension between central and local interests is still apparent. In the latter half of the 1980s, particularly after 1988, the center began to push for more standardized administration. The central regulations that the ICB was to implement became increasingly more detailed and left less room for cadre discretion. For example, the 1988 regulations on *siying qiye* were much more detailed than earlier regulations on *getihu*, and in themselves ostensibly removed one of the major gray areas in private sector administration. But many cadres appear to be resisting efforts to turn them into Weberian bureaucrats. When central regulations are not fully implemented, the ICB typically offers the excuses that its staff are insufficient or inadequately trained, or that the private business sector is too scattered and difficult to keep track of. There is some truth to these claims, but the ICB officers in places I have visited have not appeared particularly harried and overworked, and all the evidence points to ICB cadres having extensive knowledge of, and power over, businesses in their area.

Of course, the administration of such a rapidly growing and changing market sector is an extremely difficult task, but an additional interpretation of the ICB's failure fully to implement central directives lies in the contradiction between general reform imperatives of local development and regulatory efforts to constrain private business, and between the local authority developed by administrators and the central government's attempt to reduce them to mere functionaries. In the ICB, just as in local governments, local relationships matter. Inspections by ICB cadres have often been rendered ineffective by the pressure of personal connections, since inspectors are responsible for a particular area. This enables them to become very familiar with businesses in their district and to have a very clear idea of which are law-abiding and which are not. At this point, however, the complex system of *guanxi* (part personal obligation, part local loyalties) comes into play. Local officials might therefore aim not so much to eradicate illegal businesses, or to force businesses to operate in the way central authorities would like, but rather to seek an equilibrium, an arrangement mutually satisfactory to all sides wherein administrators regularly collect fines or demand that entrepreneurs contribute to their communities, and businesses meet these requirements and carry on.

As the private sector re-emerged in the 1980s, private entrepreneurs of all kinds were unusual in Chinese society in that they were independent of the majority of structures through which the state was accustomed to maintaining social control. Until the post-Mao reforms, the trend of organization in China was to make individuals part of groups—work units, communes, residential areas, the party, and Youth League—and to use these groups to control people's lives by making them reliant on them for their economic security and future advancement. For urban residents this subordination to groups had become most advanced —not only payment for work, but also housing, health care, old age security, and future career prospects all depended on the work unit, the street committee, the party. Private entrepreneurs, by virtue of being denied access to these benefits, were also immune to the leverage normally applied in this way. The reforms to agriculture and the rise of free market trade gave new flexibility to rural residents, and the existence of a legal or illegal free market in most of the necessities of life, including employment, reduced the effectiveness of these levers throughout society.

Administrative departments responded to the independence of the private sector by trying to organize private operators in such a way as to make normal procedures applicable to them: to make them part of groups. This was aimed both at facilitating control and at overcoming the perception of private operators as outcasts, separated from the collective society. This perception was seen as a barrier to the development of private business and as one reason for illicit business practices, the argument being that if private operators were imbued with a sense of belonging, they would be much more public-spirited and less inclined to cheat their customers and evade taxes. Thus administrative departments focused their activities on reducing the social marginality of private businesspeople, seeing this as the key to controlling them effectively. This approach did have some success, but was hampered by private operators' reluctance to be organized in a bureaucratic way and the lack of incentives for them to participate actively once they had been. Although the organizational methods used provided a structure for control, it was without the leverage needed to make it really effective. When it did work, it often merely created a new setting for networking between private operators and local administrators, which was effective mainly at achieving goals common to both.

A major strategy in the ICB's efforts to control private entrepreneurs was its setting up of the Individual Laborers' Association (ILA), an organization built along the lines of other "mass organizations" like the Women's Federation or trade unions, and under the control of the ICB itself. The ILA was the ICB's approximation of a *danwei* (work unit) for private businesses. In spite of its name, larger businesses were included as well as individual businesses proper, regardless of their registered status, although with the official acceptance of *siying qiye* in 1988 there came moves to set up a Private Entrepreneurs' Association specifically for them.[6] The ILA was established piecemeal, beginning at county and urban district level in 1980 under the auspices of ICB departments.[7] By the middle of 1985, 91 percent of counties and municipalities had set up these associations.[8] Then in December 1986, a national meeting of association representatives marked the establishment of the national ILA, which had been approved by the State Economic Commission in July.[9] At the meeting, the representatives "unanimously adopted" Central Committee Advisory Commission Deputy Chairman Bo Yibo as honorary president and the then director of the national ICB, Ren Zhonglin, as president.[10]

The ILA is funded out of the administration charge collected from private businesses by the ICB. In Guangzhou in 1988, 40 percent of the administration fee was allocated to the association.[11] At both national and lower levels, the association is run by committees made up partly by ICB cadres and partly by elected representatives. It is generally the ICB cadres who control the association's finances, and the association's offices are located with those of the ICB. In the national association in 1988, the finance department was run by nine people, of whom the senior three were central ICB cadres. In Guangzhou, ICB cadres acted as district secretaries, and the finances were managed directly by the ICB. The day-to-day activities of the association are organized mostly at county or district level, and most committee members are private operators, elected by members. Participation in the committee is time-consuming, but some operators see it as a way of establishing a good relationship with ICB cadres, keeping abreast of policy developments and market information, and enhancing their own power and prestige. In Chengdu, committee members are paid an honorarium for each meeting.

According to the national ILA's Beijing headquarters in 1988, the main aim of association activities was to unite, educate, and supervise private operators. Materials pertaining to business regulations and business ethics were disseminated from the central level down to the county and district level, and thence to small study groups. In some areas broadcasts or blackboards in markets were also used, particularly in small towns where association groups were not well organized. As well as disseminating propaganda and information among private business people, the association organized activities designed to mobilize them to conform to administrative goals. The Beijing municipal government's March 1983 notice on strengthening the administration of individual businesses underlined this role of the association in Item 8, which said "One important task of individual laborers' associations is to carry out regular education among individual business people in obeying the law, actively promote the *wu jiang si mei* and *san reqing* movements (both movements to promote better manners), and promote civilized business and civilized production."[12] As part of the drive to clean up free market trading in 1983 ILAs combined with the Youth League in many areas to organize a campaign among young private operators to "win the people's trust" through good service, promoting socialism, studying hard, obeying the law, displaying licenses, and helping in the fight against unlicensed traders.[13]

The ILA clearly had some success in uniting and organizing private operators and improving the ICB's links with them, but it was not without problems. Some of these arose because, again, it was an attempt to make private operators fit the administration, rather than the other way around. In most cases, association branches were organized by locality, combining private businesses of all types and sizes together. As Ole Bruun has pointed out, from the ICB's point of view this made sense: it saw them as a sociopolitical category of people whose main feature was not being part of a social unit, rather than dividing them in economic terms.[14] Organizing them by area also accorded with the normal structures of Chinese administration. As the organization of association branches built up this was criticized, and in some areas branches were organized by trade. Another problem was that although it put an administrative structure in place over private operators, the association lacked effective power over them. It could publicize policies and regulations, but it could not force operators, or indeed administrators, to obey them. It also appears to have had trouble attracting participation in some areas. Although membership in this "voluntary" association was generally automatic on obtaining a license, many operators took little interest, seeing the association—with reason—as merely an arm of bureaucracy. Others were too busy, or too mobile, to be interested in taking part. Therefore, although glowing press reports and interviews with association officials describe an organization active among nearly all private operators, most of those I have interviewed express little interest in the association or its activities. Further weight was given to this impression in a 1988 interview with staff of the Guangdong Insurance Company, who dismissed the association as quite useless as an avenue for promoting insurance or superannuation policies among private businesses.[15]

The ICB uses this organization to publicize government policies and regulations and to assist in the policing and taxation of private businesses. Thus to some extent it is dependent on private operators themselves to assist it in controlling the private sector. This often works quite well, as the ICB and the more professional private entrepreneurs have a common interest in raising standards and reducing illegality and corruption in business. However, it also gives some leverage to the entrepreneurs who cooperate with the ICB in running the association. The ICB is reliant on their assistance, and there is naturally potential for them to use their position to benefit themselves. Involvement in the ILA can be a way for an entrepreneur to build up a useful relationship with local administrators, not only in the ICB, but in street committees and the Tax Bureau as well, since they also use the association to assist them in their administrative tasks.[16] For example, the businesswoman described in chapter 5, who had left her state job to escape birth control sanctions, had used the association as a vital means of building up *guanxi*. Without, apparently, any special connections to start with, she had built up her multimillion-yuan clothing and knitting-wool business from a single stall, was a joint investor with the local ICB in a new warehouse facility, and although everyone knew she was the sole owner of her company, still had it registered as a collective. I was not able to obtain the exact details of how all this was done, but it was clear that a major factor was her apparently calculated decision to align herself with the ICB. She took an active role in the ILA and in the administration and development of the market in which her early stalls operated. She spoke of this involvement as far too time-consuming, but "necessary." It was the key to building up a good relationship with ICB cadres, keeping well-informed on policy developments, and gaining power and prestige in the market. By 1988, with her involvement in the warehouse project, she and the ICB were openly partners with a common goal.

Nor is the ILA, expanded in 1988 to include associations for operators of *siying qiye* as well, entirely a one-way mechanism for ICB control. The unusual independence of private entrepreneurs makes them more difficult to manipulate—for example, many are simply not interested in the association, and they are not in a work unit situation where they can be easily organized into taking part. In order to attract them, the association has to offer more than just political education. This, plus the ICB's interest in promoting economic reform, has meant that the association has often acted as a genuine advocate for private entrepreneurs. In spite of the original purposes of the association, there is potential for it to become quite a significant lobby for private sector interests.

As yet, though, this has been true only when these have coincided with the interests of the ICB. Efforts to improve the security and status of private business were also part of the administrative strategy of making private operators more controllable by attacking their marginality. The association assisted private operators by helping them negotiate with administrative departments other than the ICB, for example in matters of premises or supplies. It helped them obtain loans from banks, and some branches organized mutual aid funds among members, which provided welfare funds or low-interest loans funded by members' contributions. It also organized classes in business management or, more commonly, in technical skills such as hairdressing or tailoring. All these activities suited the aims of the ICB in promoting the development of a stable, manageable, and professional private sector. The association's complaints about random fees and charges have received wide publicity, but this is also a major concern of the central government and the ICB. At the inaugural meeting of the national association in December 1986, representatives were extremely vocal in voicing the complaints and desires of private operators, complaining of social prejudice and too much arbitrary bureaucratic interference, and calling for the proper implementation of central regulations. But again, this seems to have been a centrally orchestrated attack on lower-level bureaucratic obstruction of private business, prompted partly by the falls in private business numbers in the first half of 1986.[17] Bo Yibo declared that the policy of promoting the individual economy would continue, and Zhao Ziyang was pictured on the front page of the *Renmin ribao* shaking hands with private business representatives.

Taxation

China's leadership realized that the impact of market reforms made established administrative procedures inappropriate. A consistent theme in the reforms has been the desire to establish a more standardized system that relies on impersonal regulation and legality rather than the highly personalized, arbitrary system inherited from the Maoist era.[18] Yet the introduction of economic reforms before political or administrative reforms meant that economic incentives and opportunities developed before new means for regulating them were in place. As a result, the existing bureaucracies have taken hold of these opportunities and made them their own and thus have had an interest in obstructing central government efforts to standardize administration. An example of this process is the central government's efforts to develop the taxation (one of the "economic levers" much vaunted by reform economists) of the private sector.

Through the 1980s, private businesses were officially subject to an income tax and a turnover or product tax where appropriate. In addition to these central taxes, they were asked to pay the wide and varied range of local fees and levies, discussed in chapter 3, which were in many cases the main contribution of private business to local revenue. Thus it was in the interest of local governments to emphasize the collection of these local fees and charges ahead of central taxes.[19] For the central government, the implementation of a centrally regulated tax system is essential if the economy is to be successfully managed from the center, but even local-level tax bureaus, which might be seen as representing the central government, appear to have resisted the standardization of tax collection. Local loyalties were institutionalized by the fiscal contracting system, and cadres responsible for tax collection, both within the Tax Bureau bureaucracy and in township and village governments, have sought to maintain the procedures that give them the greatest degree of power in relation to both private businesses and the central government.

When individual businesses were first revived no income tax rules had been designed specifically for them; official policy was to tax them according to the fourteen-grade collective tax regulation plus an additional percentage levied on high incomes.[20] However, at this stage the government's main concern was to promote the rapid development of individual business and overcome bureaucratic prejudice and discrimination against it. In October 1980, therefore, the Ministry of Finance put out a notice declaring that the tax burden on individual businesses was too heavy and that payment according to the fourteen-grade regulation was to be discontinued.[21] Instead, income tax on individual businesses was to be decided at the provincial level in accordance with local conditions, until a national tax policy on the individual economy was formulated. It was not until 1986 that a set of regulations applying specifically to individual businesses was released. In the meantime, provinces developed their own approaches, based on the 1964 eight-level tax schedule for collective handcraft enterprises. According to economist Fang Sheng, this meant that the average income tax on individual enterprises fell by 70 percent.[22] Thus central approval was given for the development of localized and highly varied procedures for the taxation of individual businesses. Local departments sometimes used this freedom to set extremely high tax rates.[23] In October 1981, further steps were taken to lighten the tax burden, thus individual businesses in trades that the state wished to promote, or that had financial difficulties, could have their taxes waived.[24] Since larger private enterprises that exceeded the limits of *getihu* were not officially acknowledged until 1987, separate tax policies could hardly be formulated for them and it was up to local officials to deal with them as they saw fit; they were usually taxed according to their registration as *getihu*, cooperative, or collective.

During these early years, the main trend of central government policy was to promote the individual economy and overcome opposition to it. By 1983, the individual economy had grown greatly and, as reflected by the campaigns discussed above, more attention was paid to controlling it. In the field of taxation, this was seen in a switch from concern that individual businesses were being taxed too heavily, to declarations that they were not being taxed nearly enough because of their ability to evade what taxes there were. In August, the Ministry of Finance announced procedures for collecting commercial tax from individual businesses and some collectives through the wholesale units from which they bought their supplies.[25] But this was unpopular because, having been given a stake in their own profits by the reforms to state enterprise budgeting, wholesalers were now anxious not to discourage private business custom.[26] A follow-up regulation in January 1984 suggested that even those wholesalers who had been active in collecting the tax had probably had their own motives, as they had sometimes been overzealous in their role as tax agents, collecting "income tax" (although how they could possibly assess it is a mystery, and it seems more likely that it was not an approved tax at all) as well as commercial tax.[27] In any case this regulation was bound to be of limited use because, as discussed in chapter 4, individual traders were increasingly finding alternatives to state-controlled supply channels.

The main strategy for improving tax collection, as for other aspects of private sector administration, was to rely on the familiar methods of the campaign. First, in 1983 more and more complaints appeared in the press that individual traders were evading taxes by not registering for taxation, keeping false accounts, underreporting turnover, and, on occasion, beating up tax collectors.[28] In October 1983, the Tax Bureau gave further impetus to the tax collection campaign with a notice saying that individual businesses must pay tax according to the law. The notice stipulated that individual businesses must keep account books and provide evidence of turnover, income, and expenditure. Individuals who evaded tax or who refused to pay and beat up tax officials would be fined or taken to court.[29] A nationwide push for better tax inspection and collection had begun.

In succeeding years, central initiatives on tax collection followed the same trend of introducing measures aimed at making taxation more systematic and standardized, accompanied by campaigns putting pressure on officials to carry them out. In January 1986, the State Council at last issued the first national post-reform regulations on income tax on individual businesses.[30] Tax collection according to these regulations was apparently a model of order and rationality, in which the operator's taxable income was determined on the basis of the business's books and taxed according to a schedule that, for most businesses, would result in a tax burden far less than that of collective enterprises. One flaw in this scenario, however, was revealed by the issue in September of yet another declaration that individual businesses must keep books,[31] indicating that many still did not do so. Apart from this, the picture presented by central taxation policies toward individual businesses was at last one of reasonable order.

The taxation of the larger *siying qiye* was more of a problem because of the great confusion in the registration of these enterprises and because political considerations meant that their very existence was not openly discussed for several years. The taxation schedule proposed for individual businesses was in many ways unsuitable for larger enterprises, making no allowance for depreciation of assets, investment, or any differentiation between the owner's income and that of the enterprises. The common practice of taxing them as collectives was also undesirable, as it gave them access to "undeserved" tax breaks and did not provide the control over private incomes or investment levels that was necessary if socialism was to be maintained. Until the existence of large private enterprises was acknowledged and approved, no specific regulations regarding them could be formulated, and this gave rise to increasing complaints from administrators, social scientists, and private entrepreneurs themselves. Finally, the June 1988 regulations on *siying qiye* were accompanied by regulations on income tax on private enterprises and on personal income from private enterprises.[32] These regulations taxed *siying qiye* at a flat rate of 35 percent and offered strong tax incentives to enterprise expansion and investment of profits, with a provision that no less than 50 percent of after-tax profits had to be used for "production development": expansion of the enterprise, offsetting losses, paying off debts, or investing in other enterprises.[33] Apart from this stipulation, no limit was placed on the income investors might derive from the enterprise. Directors' salaries were limited to no more than ten times average staff wages and were liable to graduated personal income tax, but the portion of after-tax profits used for personal consumption was subject only to a 40 percent proportional tax.[34]

The above account of the evolution of central taxation regulation makes the process sound a little slow and disorganized, but at least the regulations themselves, once arrived at, were clear enough. A set of national standards had been achieved. Yet continued reports and academic studies on problems in taxation, and interviews with taxation officials and private entrepreneurs, give quite a different picture, of a complexity almost impenetrable not only to researchers but to businesspeople themselves. While the regulations indicate an attempt on the part of central authorities to evolve standardized, reliable procedures, the actual practice of tax collection shows a reluctance at lower levels to implement such a regulated system. Tax officials say that the conditions for such a system are lacking and rely instead on the more familiar hierarchical, group-oriented systems, which offer the greatest scope for local discretionary powers.

Urban Tax Collection: Chengdu

Officials from the tax bureaus of Sichuan Province and the city of Chengdu, interviewed in 1988, described a system of calculating and collecting tax that bore little relation to central regulations. To my initial inquiry as to how *getihu* income taxes were calculated, a provincial tax official answered that it was very straightforward: the income tax on individual businesses was calculated according to the 1986 regulations. When pressed as to how this was done without proper bookkeeping by all businesses, he added the small qualification that the regulations were applied only to the 8 percent of businesses with proper accounts. The remaining 92 percent were taxed quite differently using the *ding'e* method, in which businesses were required to pay a predetermined amount each month. The commercial tax and income tax were determined together as a set percentage of turnover, which was estimated by tax officials on the basis of their knowledge of the businesses in their area and operators' declared turnover and profit. At the Chengdu municipal Tax Bureau, the story became more complex. Several methods of tax collection were described, but the main method was as follows: individual operators were supposed to declare their earnings, but the Tax Bureau had little faith in their honesty. Businesses were therefore organized into groups according to trade, and occasional meetings were held by the Tax Bureau at which a figure for average turnover would be thrashed out. Finally, the Tax Bureau would decide on the figure to be used. This done, the amount of tax to be paid was calculated according to regulations.

For income tax, the net income was often estimated according to the gross profit rate of state enterprises in comparable lines of business, with allowance made for costs, which included purchases and expenses, government charges, the turnover tax, and salaries including that of the license holder. Income tax was then calculated according to the 1986 regulations.

According to tax officials, the amounts concerned were negotiated with operators so that they did not feel unfairly treated and were happy to pay the tax. But according to businesspeople themselves, they were given little say in the matter; they were simply told how much they were expected to pay. Most had no idea how their tax bill was arrived at, but simply paid up. Without clear bookkeeping, the system of tax calculation, if there really was one, left the Tax Bureau almost unlimited opportunity to alter the figures at will.

The actual methods of collection were similarly open to manipulation. The Tax Bureau itself did not have adequate staff to conduct all inspection and collection by itself, and therefore, again turning to well-tried methods developed since 1949, had delegated some of the burden to the ICB, the ILA, and the street committees. In Chengdu, in response to the central push for more effective tax collection in 1983, mutual supervision groups were set up, managed by representatives from street committees and the ILA, with Tax Bureau cadres supervising. Thus the street committees and the ILA acted as agents for the Tax Bureau and received either a small commission on tax collected or a bonus if cases of tax evasion were discovered. By 1986 more than six hundred such groups had been formed in Chengdu. In addition, the Tax Bureau set up inspection teams to conduct spot checks on businesses and to make estimates of average earnings, and in 1988, in response to yet more concern about tax evasion, a special task force was set up to crack down on tax evaders.

The Tax Bureau's approach to tax collection was therefore a combination of the two methods alluded to earlier: concerted inspection drives and the use of the established hierarchies of bureaucratic control. The drive approach became institutionalized, with an annual campaign reaching a peak in September–October each year, followed by press reports of successes in the crackdown on tax evasion. The very repetition of the campaign approach illustrates that the tax collection system itself was far from satisfactory. The Tax Bureau acknowledged this and attributed it to the scattered, independent nature of private businesses, inadequate tax personnel, and the fact that the majority of businesses did not keep reliable books. Yet in spite of continued central announcements on the need for individual businesses to keep books, it appears that up to 1988 no real effort had been made to make them do so. This suggests that lower-level tax officials were in fact quite satisfied with the alternative complex, arbitrary methods that left far more discretion in their hands than would a clearer and more regulated system. Tax officials admitted that they were more lenient with businesses that were seen as cooperative, honest, and socially useful, and that they applied higher taxes to those that were suspected of cheating either the state or consumers.[35] The very localized system of tax collection and the delegation of collection to members of the street committees and the ILA, who were on familiar terms with business operators on their beat, would also offer immense scope for both victimization and favoritism on the basis of graft and bribery. It also appears that other bureaucracies, such as the ICB, may not have been cooperating with the Tax Bureau in ensuring that all taxable businesses came under its control. In Chengdu in 1988, for example, only 46.1 percent of registered private businesses were paying tax to the bureau.[36]

Rural Businesses

Rural tax collection shows even clearer indications of a preference for local interests. Although the exact circumstances vary widely from place to place, a common trend is for local governments to protect the private sector from centrally regulated taxes in order to leave more funds available for the local fees and levies discussed in chapter 3.

Under the fiscal contracting system, townships and villages themselves were responsible for collecting and remitting revenue. Given a quota to fill, they usually had some freedom to choose how they filled it: in three Sichuan counties I visited in early 1992, industry had taken over from agriculture to the extent that the local governments paid their agricultural tax quotas from enterprise revenue as well. The behavior of these local governments bore out the theory of "local state corporatism" put forward by Jean Oi and others, that Chinese rural governments run their economies like a corporation, shoring up the liabilities of one enterprise or sector with the profits of another. In another example from the 1992 visit, one village filled its entire tax quota from the taxes paid by one unusually large and successful private enterprise.

That they were able to do this was indicative of the almost total local control of revenue collection from enterprises and the inability of private enterprises to protect themselves against it. The continuous complaints from the Tax Bureau and in the national and provincial press about tax evasion by private businesses apply to rural areas as well as the cities and are countered in the same way, with arguments that tax collection from private businesses is too difficult and personnel are inadequate to the task. Indeed it is true that actually implementing the details of tax regulations on private business is far beyond the resources of most rural areas, especially if there are many small family businesses. In one of the townships visited in 1992, the thriving private sector appeared to have a disproportionately light tax burden, making up 70 percent of the township's gross sales income and 57 percent of gross output value, but only paying 30 percent of tax revenue.[37] One of the ways local authorities were supporting private business, they said, was not to bother much about taxing it. But, as discussed in chapter 3, the higher-level accusations of tax evasion are matched by just as many reports of local authorities exacting myriad unofficial, even illegal, fees and collections from private businesses.

The New Drive for Central Control, 1988–1989

The tax drive of 1989, in the context of the June crackdown, sought to change this situation. It was unusually determined, and cadres in other organizations besides the Tax Bureau appear to have been given definite signals that this time the central government was serious. In Chengdu, the proportion of private businesses registered with the Tax Bureau increased to 75.5 percent by the end of September 1989, and even though more than forty thousand businesses (16 percent of the city's total in 1988) closed down, the volume of taxes collected increased from 35.2

million yuan in 1988 to over 40 million yuan by the end of September 1989.[38] Chengdu's experiences seem fairly typical, and the newspapers of early 1990 are full of reports of increased tax collection from private businesses.

The 1989 campaign was more successful than its predecessors because of the unusual political tension of the time, but it did not change the basic pattern of tax collection established in previous years. In the first half of 1989 there was already increasing publicity about tax evasion among private entrepreneurs as part of the conservative campaign against certain aspects of the reform program. Estimates of tax evasion among private operators were now high: for example, *Jingji ribao* reported in March that 60 to 70 percent of private businesses avoided paying some of their proper tax burden.[39] On 1 August, the Tax Bureau launched its collection campaign with the usual sort of notice, saying, among other things, that private operators must cooperate with tax inspectors, keep accounts according to regulations, and issue receipts.[40] Then in September, the State Council stepped up the tax collection campaign by issuing a circular on improving the taxation of private businesses.[41] The circular included the interesting provision that any dereliction of duty on the part of tax collectors ("cases related to tax inspection order") should be dealt with within the Tax Bureau itself. But already, the Tax Bureau had prepared its defenses. Tax Bureau head Jin Jin echoed his colleagues in other bureaucracies when he complained in July that the bureau had insufficient staff (one tax inspector for one hundred businesses) and added:

> Governments and departments in some places have not completely and correctly grasped the party's policy toward the individual economy, and on occasion only talk about "beneficial," not about "supplement"; they only talk about "development," not about "appropriate," and are only concerned that tax collection will damage the enthusiasm of individual businesspeople. Thus they do not sufficiently recognize the importance of improving private business tax control, and do not give it strong support.[42]

There is certainly some evidence that this was the case in the 1989 campaign. In spite of its vehemence, it was still a traditional drive organized in the usual way and dependent on local officials. Local governments and tax officials, while fulfilling the demands of the campaign, sought in some cases to defend private business from higher central tax payments and from greater central control. The impact of vested interests in the private sector was made clear in the clean-up campaign of 1989, when the drive to force fake collectives to register as private enterprises was actively obstructed by local government cadres; for example, tax officials in Liaoning were of the opinion that registering and taxing private enterprises as such could not be done as it would cause them to go bankrupt.[43] In Shenyang, a city that had actively developed the private sector, cadres apparently assisted private enterprises to defend themselves against the feared conservative attack by allowing new bogus registrations: a 21.03 percent drop in the number of registered *siying qiye* coincided with a 30 percent increase in new collective enterprises, mostly, it was claimed, the ex–*siying qiye*.[44] Figure 1.1 in chapter 1 (page 8) also suggests that the impact of the campaign was stronger in urban areas and that township and village officials may also have sought to protect private businesses.

This did not mean, however, that local cadres did not use the conservative political atmosphere to increase their own control over private business. The ICB conducted an exhaustive license inspection campaign from early 1989, and, once the campaign to extract more funds from private business had died down, there were numerous complaints that the practice of exacting random and excessive fees from private operators was increasing.[45] As discussed in chapter 3, fees and levies decided at the local level were a major source of local revenue and are clearly still a major bone of contention between local and central authorities. Although this is a question that requires further research, the central government's 1990 and 1991 declarations against such charges, and continuing problems with the registration and taxation systems, suggest that the 1989 clean-up campaign, far from being a successful assertion of central control, may have been hijacked by local authorities and used to their advantage. At the time of writing in early 1994, the government is attempting major reforms to the taxation and fiscal systems, including replacing fiscal contracting with a system in which the major enterprise taxes will be collected by the central government and redistributed to localities. One aim of this is simply to increase central government revenue, but the fiscal contracting system itself allowed local governments so much economic independence that it was a major contributor to declining central control. It is far from certain, however, that local governments will meekly give up the powers gained in the 1980s, and there are reports of widespread local efforts to resist effective implementation of the new system.[46]

Conclusion

An examination of the administration of the private business sector shows many different forces at work and in conflict with one another. In general, the ICB has been keen to promote the development of private business, but has done so in a way designed to augment its own bureaucratic power in relation to both businesses and other bureaucracies. This aim has at times conflicted with that of improving economic stability and order, as it has led to a reluctance to discard group-oriented, organizational approaches for more standardized methods, relying on clearly determined procedures and regulations. The same conflict is even more obvious in the Tax Bureau, which has had less of a commitment to promoting the private economy. Here the commonly noted conflict between central and local interests is particularly obvious, as a more standardized system would be in the interests of the central government by increasing its direct control, whereas the system of local tax calculation and collection established during the 1980s left control almost entirely in local hands.

Notes

1. *Beijing Review*, no. 33 (18 August 1980), p. 4.
2. Anders Åslund, *Private Enterprise in Eastern Europe*, p. 211. Åslund uses the term to describe the condition of the private sector arising from the combination of persistent demand for the goods and services the private sector provides, and the necessity under socialist governments for it to break or bend the law in order to survive.
3. This is part of the development that Oi, in "Fate of the Collective," refers to as "collective corporatism" on the part of rural local governments. Vivienne Shue, in *The Reach of the State*, discusses in some detail the forms of local government control under the reforms and under Mao. The evidence on private business suggests that local cadres are resisting the central government's efforts to regulate their administrative role somewhat more successfully than Shue's essays predict.
4. A 1993 *ZGGSB* article likened the private sector to a "battlefield" in the "power economy," as numerous departments fought for their share of rights to revenue from private businesses. *ZGGSB*, 12 August 1993, p. 3.
5. See, for example, the changing, even competing roles of the ICB and the Ministry of Commerce as ICB-sponsored private markets took over an increasing portion of urban vegetable marketing, in Andrew Watson, "Conflict Over Cabbages."
6. Reports of these associations present them as a spontaneous movement on the part of large-scale private entrepreneurs (*RMRB* overseas edition, 18 January 1988, p. 1; *JJRB*, 8 May 1989, p. 1; Zhang and Qin, "Siying jingji"). But then, that was the story with the ILA, too. The involvement of the ILA and the Private Entrepreneurs' Association in government policy promotion suggest that they are much the same thing, and in many localities they share offices and leading personnel. See *JJRB*, 28 April 1990, p. 2.
7. Marcia Yudkin reports, based on her interviews with ICB officials, that at least the first such organization, in Harbin, was a spontaneous move by private businesspeople themselves, later taken over by the ICB. Given the extremely tenuous position of private business at that time and the ICB's normally flexible use of terms like "spontaneous" and "voluntary," this seems unlikely.
8. *RMRB*, 14 October 1985, p. 2.
9. *RMRB*, 30 July 1986, p. 2.
10. *RMRB*, 6 December 1986, p. 2.
11. Interview, Guangzhou ICB, October 1988.
12. "Beijing shi renmin zhengfu guanyu jiaqiang dui geti gongshangyehu guanli de tongzhi," 10 March 1983, in *Zhonghuo renmin gongheguo guowuyuan gongbao* (Bulletin of the State Council of the People's Republic of China), no. 7 (1983), pp. 254–56.
13. *RMRB*, 27 February 1983, p. 1; 14 August 1983, p. 1.
14. Bruun, *Business and Bureaucracy*, p. 113. Bruun gives a detailed ac-

count of the association's relationship with private operators in Chengdu.

15. Interview, October 1988.

16. Involvement in the ILA is therefore one way in which entrepreneurs, normally outside the regular paths to official approval, can be "activists" of the sort described in state industry by Andrew Walder in his book *Communist Neo-Traditionalism.*

17. *RMRB,* 27 September 1986, p. 2; 28 December 1986, p. 2.

18. See the discussion in Victor Nee, "Peasant Entrepreneurship and the Politics of Regulation in China," and Shue, *Reach of the State.*

19. For example, the amount of revenue actually reported to higher levels will usually be much lower than the real total. See Odgaard, "Collective Control," pp. 111–13.

20. The fourteen-grade schedule, and several provincial eight-grade schedules introduced after 1978, are translated in Muth, *Private Business,* pp. 225–26.

21. "Caizheng bu guanyu gaijin hezuo shangdian he geti jingji jiaona gongshang suode shui wenti de tongzhi" (Ministry of Finance notice on improving the payment of industrial and commercial income tax by cooperative shops and the individual economy), 9 October 1990, in Guojia gongshang xingzheng guanli ju geti jingji si and *Beijing ribao* lilun bu, eds., *Geti laodongzhe shouce,* pp. 48–49.

22. Fang, "Revival of the Individual Economy," p. 183.

23. Solinger, *Chinese Business,* p. 203.

24. *RMRB,* 29 April 1985, p. 2. *Beijing Review,* no. 44 (2 November 1981), p. 27, stated that new individual and collective enterprises would be exempt from commercial tax for three years, but the reports of early taxation practices by Yudkin, *Making Good,* pp. 84–85, suggest that this was not always so. I have found no cases of such exemptions except for certain repair or service businesses seen by local authorities as not very profitable but highly beneficial to the community.

25. "Caizheng bu guanyu dui geti shangfan he bufen jiti shangye qiye shixing you pifa bumen daikou lingshou huanjie gongshang shui de zanxing guiding" (Ministry of Finance provisional regulations on the collection of retail-level industrial and commercial tax on individual peddlers and some collective commercial enterprises through wholesale departments), 17 August 1983, in *Zhonghua renmin gongheguo guowuyuan gongbao,* no. 18 (1983), pp. 832–34.

26. *RMRB,* 2 September 1989, p. 6.

27. "Caizheng bu guanyu dui geti shangfan he bufen jiti shangye qiye you pifa bumen daikou shuikuan jige wenti de tongzhi" (Ministry of Finance notice on several problems in the collection of taxes from individual peddlers and some collective commercial enterprises by wholesale departments), 10 February 1984, in *Zhonghua renmin gongheguo guowuyuan gongbao,* no. 5 (1984), p. 159.

28. For example, *RMRB,* 16 July 1983, p. 3; *Ha'erbin ribao,* 13 July 1983, p. 1.

29. "Zhonghua renmin gongheguo caizheng bu shuiwu ju guanyu geti

gonshangyehu bixu yifa nashui de tongzhi" (Notice of the Tax Bureau of the People's Republic of China Ministry of Finance: individual businesses must pay tax according to the law), 8 October 1983, in Guojia gongshang xingzheng guanliju geti jingji si and *Beijing ribao* lilun bu, eds., *Geti laodongzhe shouce*, pp. 46–47.

30. "Zhonghua renmin gongheguo chengxiang geti gongshangyehu suode shui zanxing tiaoli" (People's Republic of China provisional regulations on income tax on urban and rural individual industrial and commercial households), 7 January 1986, in *RMRB*, 25 January 1986, p. 2.

31. *JJRB*, 15 September 1986, p. 2.

32. "Zhonghua renmin gongheguo siying qiye suode shui zanxing tiaoli" (People's Republic of China provisional regulations on private enterprise income tax), 3 June 1988; and "Guowuyuan guanyu zhengshou siying qiye touzizhe geren shouru tiaojie shui de guiding" (Decision of the State Council on the collection of regulatory personal income tax from investors in private enterprises), in *RMRB*, 29 June 1988.

33. After the release of these regulations, the Tax Bureau also levied a 7 percent "accumulation tax," to be used for centrally funded transport and construction projects. See *Xinwen bao* (News), 27 July 1989.

34. On the face of it, these regulations appeared to give many owners of large *siying qiye* significant advantages over both *getihu* and collective enterprises. A collective enterprise with an income of more than 25,000 yuan should, according to the relevant regulations, have been taxed at progressive rates over 42 percent, and the provisions for directors' salaries, covering losses, and further investment are likely to provide useful loopholes. In fact, most *siying qiye* would be considerably worse off if taxed as such, which is another reason why they prefer to be registered as something else. Many private enterprises registered as collectives were in fact being taxed at an unofficial proportional rate of around 20 percent, or received tax concessions such as a tax-free period of up to three years designed to encourage the development of collective township enterprises. The new regulations also meant that an entrepreneur's personal income would be taxed twice. For discussions of these issues, see Cheng Xiangqing, Li Bojun, and Xu Huafei, "Siying qiye fazhan xianzhuang yu mianlin de wenti," and *Zhongguo shehui jieji, jieceng yanjiu* Guangzhou yanjiu zu, "Guangzhou geti gongshangye, siying qiye jingji zhuangkuang de fenxi," p. 45. For the regulations on collective enterprise income tax, see *RMRB*, 20 April 1985, p. 2.

35. Bruun, *Business and Bureaucracy*, p. 122, notes that there is some animosity toward private operators who, because of their good connections, manage to get a lower tax assessment.

36. ICB report obtained at an interview, Chengdu, January 1991. The percentage is calculated after tax-exempt businesses have been excluded.

37. Based on the figures given at an interview. When we later looked at the figures handed up to county level, the proportions roughly matched.

38. Interview, Chengdu, January 1991.

39. *JJRB*, 8 March 1989, p. 2.

40. *RMRB*, 2 August 1989, p. 2.
41. *SWB*, 5 September 1989, FE/0553 B2/7.
42. *JJRB*, 14 July 1989, p. 2.
43. *JJCK*, 15 May 1989, p. 1; Cheng, Li, and Xu, "Siying qiye," p. 29.
44. *JJCK*, 11 April 1990, p. 1.
45. See, for example, the series of letters and reports in *ZGGSB*, January–February 1991.
46. See, for example, *SWB*, 19 November 1993, FE/1850 G/6–7.

—————— 7 ——————

Into the 1990s: Reassessing the Role
of the Private Sector

The private sector was allowed to grow in response to the imperatives of economic reform and marketization, but in doing so
it developed into something both quantitatively and qualitatively
different from the small, "supplementary" sector of the simple
individual tailor or stallholder of the early promotion of the individual economy. By the late 1980s private business played an
important role in the economy and was increasingly integrated
within it, while reforms in other ownership sectors were providing increasing opportunities for private control and ownership of
productive assets. These developments, among others, made the
traditional vision of a state-controlled economy difficult to maintain, to the point that trying to define and administer the economy
according to established concepts was merely counterproductive.
The debates on the private sector and on economic reform in
general in the late 1980s and early 1990s implicitly recognized
this, and reformists began to develop a new approach that sets
aside many of the ideological concerns that colored private sector
development throughout the 1980s.

The Renewed Theoretical Debate on Private Enterprise

In the latter half of the 1980s, the need to revise the accepted
concept of the private sector in the light of the facts gave rise to a

lively debate and some energetic theoretical gymnastics in China, revolving around three key issues of employment and exploitation, income distribution, and state dominance and control of the economy. This debate reached a peak in 1987–88, but was stifled by the changed political environment after June 1989. By that time, however, the momentum of reform was such that the attempt to reassert more conservative values and control mechanisms was short lived, and following Deng Xiaoping's support for rapid reform and growth during his tour of several southern cities in early 1992, new initiatives were made to promote the private sector and confirm its legitimacy.

Exploitation

The larger private enterprises naturally provoked concern over their owners' high incomes and reliance on the labor of others.[1] As one private businessperson put it, *"yao xiang fu, jiu dei gu"* (If you want to get rich, you have to employ others),[2] but in doing so the twin specters of polarization and exploitation were evoked. One response to the growth of such enterprises was to say that they were exploitative and capitalist in nature and incompatible with socialist principles. Such arguments pointed to employers' high incomes and related these directly to the number of employees. A study of private enterprises in Tianjin, for example, reported that whereas in enterprises with seven employees the owner's income was on average 5.5 times that of employees, the difference went up in direct proportion to the number of staff until, in enterprises with more than sixty employees, owners' incomes were nearly seventy times that of employees.[3]

Critics pointed out that this type of equation takes no account of the entrepreneur's capital assets or management, but the response was that such striking disparities could not be merely the reward for the employer's allegedly more complex labor, risk, or interest on capital, but must surely be surplus value appropriated from the workers.[4] There was also much concern about income polarization and the jealousy provoked by private entrepreneurs' high incomes. A survey of private businesses in Beijing gave their reported net income as averaging 409 yuan per month; the average for those with employees was 799.63 yuan per month, 2.7 times higher.[5] A Shanghai survey reported employer incomes of generally between 5,000 and 10,000 yuan per year, with some netting 30,000–40,000 yuan. One employer in Shenyang was reported to have an annual net income of a staggering 800,000 yuan, at a time when urban per capita incomes averaged 1,119 yuan.[6]

Another line of argument admitted to a difference between small individual businesses and large employers, but maintained that the latter were still not capitalist. The employers' high incomes did arise partly from exploitation, but they themselves also participated in labor, and the relationship between employer and employee was one of mutual benefit and equality, quite different from that found in capitalist countries. The capitalist nature of the enterprise was mitigated by the surrounding socialist system.[7]

Opponents responded with reports showing that the relationship between employers and employed was in fact far from idyllic. Working hours were generally longer than those in state or collective units; payment was often by the piece-rate system, with rates lower than those in state units. Thus workers ended up with a higher salary than in state units, but only by working harder.[8] And this was not merely the extra work to be expected in an efficient enterprise with no "iron rice bowl": the longer hours could be sixteen hours a day or more.[9] Provisions for workers' safety, health, insurance, and other benefits had not been regulated and hence were often nonexistent,[10] although some employers made a point of providing good conditions to avoid being labeled as capitalist exploiters. Employment was often on a casual basis, and calls for the prohibition of child labor indicate its prevalence.[11] However, these conditions must be compared to the alternative of unemployment or perhaps contract employment in a publicly owned enterprise where conditions may be no better. In visits to both private and collective enterprises in rural Sichuan in 1992 I could find no better conditions or welfare benefits in any but the largest of the collective enterprises, and state enterprise conditions have also been rapidly eroded by contract employment and harder budget constraints. In chapter 3 it was noted that private businesspeople would often try to have some link to public enterprise employment to obtain benefits: by the early 1990s it was increasingly the case that state enterprise employees needed some link with private enterprise to obtain an acceptable income.

While some writers remained concerned about the exploitation issue, for many, finding effective means of raising general income levels seemed more important. "Exploitation," argued one scholar, "cannot be made the standard for measuring social welfare."[12] Said one group of economists in Wenzhou:

> It is foolish in the extreme to seek an unrealistic social equality at the cost of sacrificing economic efficiency. . . . Within the limits of income inequality that society will bear, the only aim should be raising efficiency and promoting economic development. And, judging from Wenzhou, society can accept much more income inequality than people think.[13]

Some commentators discarded attempts to give private enterprise a veneer of socialist respectability, saying that *siying qiye* were capitalist, but should be supported anyway.

> What we now call a "privately run economy" [*siying jingji*] is in fact a private capitalist economy [*siren zibenzhuyi jingji*]. I believe that in the initial stage of socialism private capitalist economy must be developed much more. So long as it is beneficial to the development of the forces of production, we should admit the existence of private capitalist economy and admit the existence of exploitation.[14]

Reassessment of the "Supplement" Theory

The changes in economic relationships wrought by the reforms could not fail to bring into question the original assertion that the private sector in China would consist of small family concerns, easily controlled and limited by their dependence on the publicly owned economy. From around 1985, articles began to appear in scholarly journals arguing that the "individual economy" was becoming much more than a mere supplement.[15] By 1988, however, some published articles were beginning to challenge the whole basis upon which assessments of China's ownership relations were made, defining "private" not solely in terms of nominal ownership, but also in terms of management and use rights. This meant that they included the vast majority of rural producers in their discussions of the private economy. A 1988 article in the Tianjin newspaper *Kaifa bao* (Development), for example, argued that the *"geti siying jingji"* (individual privately run economy) now basically dominated agriculture, and the prices of many commodities were no longer determined by the state. Private enterprises were moving into materials and machinery production as well as light industry; if individually leased enterprises were also taken into account, the privately run sector was much more than a "supplement." The writer also argued that since more and more of China's new jobs were being provided by this private sector, and given China's huge labor force and the reserves of labor still to be transferred from agriculture, the private sector must continue to grow. Therefore, the article concluded, the private and privately run economy "cannot be reversed, and is no longer merely a beneficial supplement subordinate to the publicly owned system, but plays an influential role in the national economy."[16]

A similar case was made by Shi Chenglin of the Changde Rural Economy Committee, Hunan, in a 1989 article published by *Nongye jingji wenti* (Problems in Agricultural Economy), entitled "A Reassessment of the 'Supplement' Theory."[17] But this article was published in February. Over a year later, the same journal published a critique of Shi's article, which clearly showed the impact of the 1989 crackdown on both the arguments made and the quality of those arguments. It doggedly ignored all the changes in management brought about by the reforms, and all the theoretical debates that had gone on before June 1989, to argue that it was impossible to call China's agricultural production "private" because the land was collectively owned. The writer then clinched the argument with the statement that the privately run economy could not possibly, ever, be more than a supplement, because China was a socialist country:

> Take the practical implications of the privately run economy: its basic nature is capitalist, and in our socialist country it cannot increase to the leading position. The socialist system will not allow it; a socialist system cannot be established upon a capitalist economic base.[18]

And that, as far as the discussion of the private sector was concerned, was that, at least for the time being. But although many Chinese scholars turned their attention to less controversial matters for a while, the private sector itself was by now well-established enough to survive the attack of 1989. After Deng Xiaoping's southern tour in early 1992, the ICB and local governments again actively promoted its development. Economic growth was restored to its position as the main criterion for policy decisions, and concerns about exploitation were largely set aside. The ICB adopted a policy of "loosening up and enlivening" its administrative procedures, and this generally meant a more flexible approach to *getihu* and *siying qiye* regulation.[19] In 1993, several provincial and municipal-level governments and ICB branches issued new guidelines on promoting both *getihu* and *siying qiye* development, with new measures including special *siying qiye* development zones, assisting private businesses to obtain credit, key personnel, technology, and links with other enterprises including foreign ones, simplifying registration procedures and categories, and including private business development in economic plans at all levels of government.[20] The active promotion of *siying qiye* indicated a more relaxed attitude to the exploitation question, and the tone of the statements issued on these occasions also differed markedly compared to the 1980s. The patronizing and ultimately restrictive references to the "supplementary" role of private business became less prominent and were replaced by references to the private sector's importance as a source of revenue and "an important economic force in developing new productive forces."[21]

On the theoretical level, renewed discussions of the role of private business again moved toward dropping the "supplement" idea. In August 1992 in Beijing, the ICB held a conference on developing the private economy at which some participants suggested that calling the private sector a "supplement" was inappropriate and that it was an integral part of "socialism with Chinese characteristics."[22] The issue of exploitation reportedly elicited a general consensus that contemporary *siying qiye* were somewhat different from capitalist enterprises in pre-revolutionary China, and even the bald proposal that operators of *siying qiye* should be allowed to join the Communist Party (this had been banned after June 1989), because "We must treat this question on the basis of the standard of the productive forces, not the standard of virtue."

Toward a New Ownership Structure

The reassessment of the private sector was part of a much wider debate on the structure of ownership under socialism and the problems of China's state sector and how to overcome them. For a start, the promotion of private and collective ownership (which meant abandoning the idea of inexorable, *upward* progression toward state ownership) challenged state ownership ideologically. The very admission that the state sector needed a "supplement" had been an acknowledgment of failure. The concept of the initial stage of socialism sought to confine the failure to past misjudgment of the historical moment, but was not convincing. By progression, the admission of shortcomings in one area inevitably raised questions about others: if the state-run sector was inappropriate for roadside noodle stalls, was it better for noodle factories? The contrast between continued poor performance in the state sector and the booming growth of the collective and private sectors could not fail to beg the question.

Therefore, the structural reform of the state–collective–private ownership mix was accompanied by reforms in the management of the public economy aimed at improving its performance. Much of the early discussion on these issues followed the "initial stage of socialism" theory and was in terms of the appropriate level of centralization (meaning ownership) for a given industry and level of productive forces. This approach was relatively tactful and face-saving, as it suggested that a state-run economy was theoretically superior—just not yet. At a more analytical level, an academic debate developed that went much further, examining the source of state enterprises' poor performance in political terms. According to some, state ownership as practiced in China was not in fact "public ownership," still less was it ownership by the workers. Enterprises and workers, having no direct right to the benefits of property or, following Kornai's theory of the soft budget constraint, to its associated risks, had no incentive to use the means of production efficiently.[23] Several theoreticians began to argue that "public ownership" in China was intrinsically inefficient because of its lack of definition: in terms of real control, an enterprise was not owned by any one body, but by an assortment of bureaucracies such as the Planning Commission, the Labor Bureau, the Price Bureau, and relevant ministries.[24] This tended to give rise to interest-group lobbying and corruption as well as a lack of real concern for the enterprise and perpetuated the personalized management of the economy by cadres rather than the systematic rule of (centrally controlled) law as favored by reformist leaders.

An increasingly popular solution to these problems is the proposal to reorganize the ownership of public enterprises into shares. Joint stock ownership has been seen as the optimum course to follow for reforming the whole economy, as it offers the benefits expected from privatization, can be effected gradually, leaves room for continued state influence through shareholding, and is seen as an "advanced" form of ownership—the pinnacle of the Western sequence of economic development that has defined the Chinese concept of modernization. It can also be presented in an ideologically acceptable way, as the shareholders can be seen as collective owners of the enterprise and there is no one capitalist "boss." Some writers have argued that joint stock ownership is a much truer form of "public ownership" than the state or collective ownership practiced in China.[25]

The movement toward reorganizing ownership in this way is of great significance to private enterprise. This is not only because of the economic opportunities it is likely to afford particular entrepreneurs but because of the political and administrative ramifications for all private businesses. Any widespread application of share ownership implies discarding the old system of categorizing and regulating the economy according to state, collective, and private ownership sectors. The established category of "joint" enterprises already includes so many different kinds of enterprise—Sino-foreign joint ventures, joint ventures between Chinese enterprises of common or differing ownership, rural share enterprises, and numerous private enterprises hiding under the "joint" label—as to be of little use. The variety of regulations and practices aimed at regulating the proportions of each ownership type in the economy are complicated to administer, often clash with one another, and are a source of statistical and administrative confusion as well as corruption, as both enterprises and local administrators seek to maximize their own advantage.

The New Approach to Central Control, 1989 and After

The role of local authorities—whether local government cadres or officials at the lower levels of vertical bureaucracies like the ICB—in developing private business in China highlights one of the major issues of the reforms: the mechanisms and extent of central control. Throughout the 1980s, private entrepreneurs remained extremely dependent on the goodwill of local cadres. Administrative controls on private business remained highly localized and subject to the discretion of officials, who manipulated private enterprise to benefit themselves or their localities or both. Vivienne Shue, in her book of essays *The Reach of the*

State, suggests that a major aim of reformists has been to break down this local leverage by increasing the role of the market and standardizing administration, turning officials into corporate executives rather than old-style cadres. Such an agenda can clearly be seen in the central government's efforts to standardize the administration of the private sector. But, at the same time, the resistance of local cadres to this reduction in their role can be seen in the way they have responded, continuing to exercise local authority and extract local levies from private business, while pleading inability to implement central regulations. When the central government's main aim was simply to promote economic growth, this did not matter too much, but in times of economic and political retrenchment, when the center sought more direct control over the economy, local interests became a major obstacle.

Meanwhile, the forces that had caused China's leadership to promote the private sector in 1978 did not diminish as reforms progressed; on the contrary, consumer demand and the need to create jobs continued to increase. By the late 1980s, the state was less able than ever to provide for all the needs of consumers; and furthermore, after a decade of reform, with its constant discussion of living standards and its openness to other countries, the public was less willing than ever to put up with its failure to do so. The private sector was part of a network of nonstate production and marketing that was of vital importance to maintaining living standards and was also of considerable value to local governments and cadres themselves. The economic and political costs of attacking it would be great.

The campaign to increase administrative control over private business that began in early 1989, and appeared to escalate into outright attack after 4 June, clearly illustrates the way the above factors continued to force those who oppose the private economy to back down. The political and economic clampdown of 1989 had grave implications for the future of private business. In many ways, the private sector epitomized the anarchic forces generated by the reform program. Private entrepreneurs were outside the regular systems of collective social control, they were difficult to police, they engaged in bribery and corrupted the publicly owned economy, they evaded taxes, and their high incomes provoked popular discontent. They were also, because of their still-marginal social position, an ideal scapegoat for some of the deep political and economic problems China was experiencing.[26]

Therefore 1989 brought renewed attempts to improve administrative control over private business in the form of a major clean-up campaign, relicensing of private operators and the most determined tax collection drive since the reforms began. After the suppression of the protest movement in June, there was also a marked change in the official publicity concerning private entrepreneurs, as traditional Marxist-Leninist ideology made a come-back. The ownership debate came to a sudden halt, and numerous newspaper articles appeared that insisted on the maintenance of the existing state–collective–private system, using Marxist rhetoric that had been absent from economic debate for years.[27] The resurrection of the Lei Feng campaign in the months after June 1989 implied a rejection of the profit-seeking, entrepreneurial behavior previously held up as a model. Official efforts to popularize private entrepreneurs and justify their high incomes disappeared. Instead, people dissatisfied with low incomes and rising prices were encouraged to direct their anger at private operators. The publicity concerning the tax collection drive now implied that most private operators derived their high incomes not from their risk, capital, and hard work as claimed before, but from tax evasion. Private businesses were also blamed for much of the corruption and black marketeering, which had become so objectionable to the public. One article spoke of an army of corrupt *getihu* undermining the integrity of the socialist economy:

> The great disparity between individual operators and staff and workers in general is one of the main indications of unequal social distribution. The high incomes of *getihu* and the ease with which they obtain them make a small number of staff and cadres "down swords" and join the ranks of the *getihu* [i.e., by accepting bribes from them].[28]

Yet the central leadership never actually revoked its support of the private sector as a limited supplement; and as we have seen, the "supplement" theory has been rendered untenable. The government news service declared in August 1989 that "the private sector will continue to develop," as this was "conducive to solving the serious employment problems by invigorating the domestic economy."[29] In October, at a national meeting on production, Li Peng reiterated that private businesses were "a necessary supplement," although he characterized them as "small businessmen and peddlers" and alluded to the need to crack down on tax evasion and illicit wholesale profits.[30] By late 1989 there was clearly concern at the decline in private sector numbers, and officials and press articles again began to offer assurances that the policy of promoting both *getihu* and *siying qiye* had not changed. In early 1990, an ICB report to the State Council noted the need to clarify further that the policies of promoting the private economy, encouraging some people to get rich first, and protecting the legal rights of *getihu* and *siying qiye*, had not been altered.[31] Although the ICB's raising of the issue indicates the strength of the attack on the private sector, the fact that it was reported in *Renmin ribao* also shows the leadership's concern that the attack should not be allowed to go too far.

In relation to both the private sector and the economy as a whole, the period after June 1989 showed that while it is possible for the central leadership to crack down severely and effectively on social and political unrest, in economic matters the old approach to state control no longer works. In the private sector, the continued insistence that the private sector be limited to a supplementary role and that the planning of the economy revolve around an ownership hierarchy had forced private entrepreneurs into illegal or semi-legal behavior. The administrative barriers created by giving preference to state and collective enterprises provided further opportunities for corruption, as economic interests arising from the reforms encouraged administrators to bend these barriers where possible. This increased the power of local administrators over private entrepreneurs, lent itself to extortion, and decreased the central government's control. Thus the attempt to preserve state control by insisting on the dominance of the state sector has been frustrated by the effect of reforms and has become self-defeating. Adherence to the "supplement" theory and the equivocal political status this implies for the private sector means that although the private sector is no longer marginal in many respects, many entrepreneurs continue to behave in a marginal way. The private sector remains characterized by a reluctance to invest in long-term projects, a high element of risk income, and conspicuous consumption. In the administration of the private sector, as in many other areas, effective economic direction now requires fundamental changes in the government's approach to economic administration. Thus, the question of ownership is inherently linked to the nature of state administration and its operation.

Reformists have long realized this, and this study of private business has shown their ideas at work in the efforts to remove restrictions on economic activity according to form of ownership, to make administration more systematic and less subject to personal discretion and to improve the taxation system. With Deng Xiaoping's support for more daring economic policies and the retreat of more conservative leaders in 1992, these efforts were resumed. The policy decisions, laws, and regulations released since the Fourteenth Party Congress, particularly surrounding the Third Plenum of the Fourteenth Central Committee in November 1993, made significant moves toward discarding ownership discrimination. The decision released by the plenum announced the intention of taking up the proposals on ownership reform in state enterprises by using shareholding systems to turn large state enterprises into independently responsible companies and continuing to lease out or sell off smaller ones. In addition, it supported further growth in the private sector and stated that "The state should create conditions for economic sectors under different kinds of ownership to compete in the market on equal terms, and should deal with the various types of enterprises without discrimination."[32] A rash of new laws and regulations are being released on companies, limited liability, shareholding, accounting proce-

dures, and taxation, which are applicable to a variety of ownership combinations.

Conclusion

How successfully the policies and regulations released since
1992 will be implemented remains to be seen, but they indicate a
fundamental reassessment of the ideology underpinning the old
approach to socialist development in China. Even if these policy
decisions are reversed or abandoned, the forces behind them
remain to be dealt with, a result of the enormous changes that
took place in China's political economy in the 1980s. The growth
of the private sector was a significant part of these changes. As
this study has shown, private entrepreneurs reacted with alacrity
to the new opportunities arising in the 1980s and interacted with
the changing reform environment to produce a dynamic, fast-
growing economic force that, from its niche at the matrix of old
power structures and new incentives, challenged many of the
assumptions on which the "planned commodity economy" was to
be built.

By their very success, the private entrepreneurs have demon-
strated the vitality of the profit motive, and the private sector has
expanded beyond the negligible role first assigned to it, forcing
changes in taxation, licensing, and regulation along the way. But
the changes have not all been in one direction. In the process of
its development, the private sector has developed complex and
intimate relationships with administrators and other ownership
sectors. This patronage has afforded it some protection, as it has
made it the subject of a quiet power struggle among both vertical
and horizontal divisions of the administrative structure. In return
for this protection, however, it has remained dependent on administrative goodwill, particularly local administrative goodwill,
and its fortunes are tied to both central political fluctuations and
local development strategies. The moves toward abandoning
ownership discrimination and strengthening central legal regulation would tend to remove many of the factors that shaped the

private sector in the 1980s, but these moves are likely to be resisted. This means that while the private sector in China is likely to continue to grow, for at least the near future it will often not be entirely "private," but will remain intimately connected to collective and administrative power structures.

Notes

1. The following section is reprinted, with some changes, from Susan Young, "Policy, Practice and the Private Sector," *Australian Journal of Chinese Affairs*, no. 21 (January 1989), pp. 69–73.

2. *JJRB*, 5 December 1987, p. 2.

3. Quoted in You Lianpu, "Shilun wo guo xian jieduan siren gugong jingji de xingzhi," p. 48.

4. *JJRB*, 5 December 1987, p. 2; Li Shi, "Wenzhou moshi de jige lilun wenti," p. 28; Wu, "Wo guo geti jingji," p. 77.

5. The figures for Beijing, Shanghai, and Shenyang were all quoted in *JJRB*, 12 February 1988, p. 1.

6. *ZTN*, 1990, p. 289.

7. Chen and Chen, "Shanghai siren jingji," p. 27; Zhang et al., " 'Wenzhou moshi,' " p. 6.

8. *Jingjixue zhoubao* (Economics Weekly), 24 January 1988, p. 3.

9. *JJRB*, 5 December 1987, p. 2.

10. *JJCK*, 1 February 1988, p. 4.

11. Hu Anchao, "Shilun wo guo siren qiye de falü diwei yu tiaozheng," p. 52; *SWB*, 10 March 1988, FE/0096 B2/4. In 1991, the State Council put out a set of regulations banning child labor: see *SWB*, 11 May 1991, FE/1096 C1/1–2.

12. Li Shi, "Wenzhou moshi," p. 28.

·13. Zhang et al., " 'Wenzhou moshi,' " p. 6.

14. Feng Lanrui at a conference on economic strategy held by the Chinese Academy of Social Sciences, November 1987. See *Jingjixue zhoubao*, 6 December 1987, p. 1. One of the more outspoken and prolific writers at this time, Xiao Liang of *Social Sciences in China*, was quite up-front about the problem: in one article, after arguing forcefully that *siying qiye* were capitalist enterprises, he noted the bad public relations effects of naming them as such, and suggested that, while theoretical analysts should be aware of the true situation, it might be better for the private sector's development prospects to go on using vague terms like *"siying jingji."* See Xiao Liang, "Guanyu siying jingji de jige lilun wenti."

15. For example, Song and Tan, "Lai zi chengshi getihu de tiaozhan," and Li and Zhao, "Geti jingji zuoyong."

16. *Kaifa bao* (Development), 15 January 1988, p. 3.

17. Shi Chenglin, "Dui 'buchong lun' de zai renshi."

18. Chen Baocai, "Dui 'buchong lun' de zai renshi yi wen de shangque," p. 45.

19. One report suggested that this had gone too far and local cadres were once again putting development ahead of orderly administrative control. See *ZGGSB*, 5 June 199, p. 3.

20. Specific measures were decided locally and varied from place to place. These examples are taken from Shanghai, Chengdu, Zhengzhou, Shenzhen, Qingdao, and Heilongjiang. See *ZGGSB*, 5 June 1993, p. 1; 15 July 1993, p. 2; 29 July 1993, p. 1; and 5 August 1993, p. 1; *Zhongguo xinxi bao* (Chinese News), 16 July 1993, p. 4.

21. *Zhongguo xinxi bao*, 16 July 1993, p. 4.

22. Huang Rutong, "Geti, siying jingji jiankang fazhan zhengce yantaohui guandian zongshu," p. 23.

23. Zhong Dong, "Shehuizhuyi xuyao siyouzhi ma?" p. 14.

24. Yang Xiaokai, "Economic Thinking and Reforms in China."

25. For example, Rong Jian and Fan Hengshan, "Lun suoyouzhi de kaifang."

26. This point is made by Anita Chan and Jonathan Unger in "Voices from the Protest Movement, Chongqing, Sichuan," p. 19.

27. *Guangming ribao*, for example, published an article entitled "On the antipeople nature of 'A declaration of private ownership,' " on 28 July 1989. This article attacked the pro-privatization sentiments expressed in a wallposter entitled "China's hope—a declaration of private ownership," which had been put up at the Institute of Aeronautics and Astronautics. The very title of the *GMRB* article recalled the class-struggle polemics of the Cultural Revolution. See *SWB*, 8 August 1989, FE/0529 B2/7, for an English summary. For further examples, see *RMRB*, 4 September 1989, p. 6; 2 December 1989, pp. 1–2.

28. *RMRB*, 2 November 1989, p. 2.

29. *SWB*, 14 August 1989, FE/0534 B2/4.

30. *SWB*, 28 October 1989, FE/0599 B2/3.

31. *RMRB*, 26 March 1990, p. 2.

32. "Decision of the CCP Central Committee on Some Issues Concerning the Establishment of a Socialist Market Economic Structure," 14 November 1993, in *SWB*, 18 November 1993, FE/1849 S1/1–15, p. S1/4.

——— Bibliography ———

Åslund, Anders. "The Functioning of Private Enterprise in Poland." *Soviet Studies* 36, no. 3 (July 1984): 427–44.

———. *Private Enterprise in Eastern Europe: The Non-Agricultural Private Sector in Poland and the GDR, 1945–83.* London and Basingstoke: Macmillan, 1985.

Barrett, Jill. "What's New in China's New Constitution?" *Review of Socialist Law* 9, no. 4 (1983): 305–45.

Benxi shi tigai ban. "Cong zulin yige shangdian fazhan wei shangye zulin jituan —ji Benxi shi dongming shangye jituan" (From leasing one shop to a commercial leasing consortium—the Dongming commercial consortium, Benxi). In *Zhongguo jingji tizhi gaige shi nian* (Ten years of structural economic reform in China), eds. Guojia jingji tizhi gaige weiyuanhui, 276–80. Beijing: Jingji guanli chubanshe, 1988.

Bonnin, Michel, and Michel Cartier. "Urban Employment in Post-Mao China." In *Transforming China's Economy in the Eighties—Vol. 1: The Rural Sector, Welfare and Employment*, eds. S. Feuchtwang, A. Hussain, and T. Pairault. Boulder, Colo.: Westview Press, 1988.

Bruun, Ole. *Business and Bureaucracy in a Chinese City: An Ethnography of Private Business Households in Contemporary China.* Berkeley: Institute of East Asian Studies, University of California, 1993.

———. "The Reappearance of the Family as an Economic Unit: A Sample Survey of Individual Households in Workshop Production and Crafts, Chengdu, Sichuan Province, China." *Copenhagen Discussion Papers*, no. 1. Copenhagen: University of Copenhagen Center for East and Southeast Asian Studies, 1988.

Byrd, William A., and Lin Qingsong, eds. *China's Rural Industry—Structure, Development, and Reform.* New York: Oxford University Press for the World Bank, 1990.

Chan, Anita, and Jonathan Unger. "Voices from the Protest Movement, Chongqing, Sichuan." *Australian Journal of Chinese Affairs*, no. 24 (July 1990): 1–21.

Chao Yü-shen. "Expansion of Individual Economy in Mainland China." *Issues and Studies* 16, no. 9 (1980): 7–10.

Chen Baocai. "Dui 'buchong lun' de zai renshi yi wen de shangque" (A discussion of the article "A reassessment of the 'supplement' theory"). *Nongye jingji wenti* (Problems in Agricultural Economics), no. 8 (1990): 45–46.

Chen Baorong and Chen Xiumei. "Shanghai siren jingji ruogan wenti tantao" (A probe into some problems concerning Shanghai's private economy). *Shehui kexue* (Social Science), no. 9 (1986): 28–42.

Chen Jianhua. "Cong wu xu dao you xu—Fujian sheng Changle xian siying qiye fazhan de diaocha" (From disorder to order—an investigation of the development of private enterprises in Changle county, Fujian). *FBZ* F22, no. 11 (1988): 41–46. First published in *Zhongguo jingji wenti* (Chinese Economic Problems), no. 5 (1988): 51–56.

Chen Rengxing. "Shilun wo guo xian jieduan de geti jingji" (A tentative discussion of China's individual economy). *Xinhua wenzhai* (New China Digest), no. 4 (1983): 60–61.

Ch'en Te-sheng. " 'Individual Economy' in Mainland China." *Issues and Studies* 23, no. 1 (1987): 8–10.

Chen Xin. "Lun siying jingji de fazhan jieduan" (The stages of development in the private economy). *Jingji yanjiu* (Economic Research), no. 9 (1989): 73–78.

Cheng Xiangqing, Li Bojun, and Xu Huafei. "Siying qiye fazhan xianzhuang yu mianlin de wenti" (Current conditions and problems in the development of private enterprises). *Zhongguo nongcun jingji* (China's Rural Economy), no. 2 (1989): 24–31.

Chinese Communist Party. "Resolution on Certain Questions in the History of Our Party since the Founding of the People's Republic of China," 27 June 1981. In *CCP Resolution on Party History*. Beijing: Foreign Languages Press, 1981.

Davis, Deborah, and Ezra Vogel, eds. *Chinese Society on the Eve of Tiananmen*. Cambridge: Harvard University Press, 1990.

de Rosario, Louise. "The Private Dilemma." *Far Eastern Economic Review* (20 November 1986): 68–69.

Dong Fureng. "Guanyu wo guo shehuizhuyi suoyouzhi xingshi wenti" (On the problem of the forms of socialist ownership in China). *Jingji yanjiu*, no.1 (1979): 21–28.

———. "Chinese Economy in the Process of Great Transformation." In *Economic Reform in the PRC*, ed. George C. Wang, 125–37. Boulder, Colo.: Westview Press, 1982.

Falü chubanshe fagui bianjibu, eds. *Siying qiye changyong falü shouce* (Handbook of laws often used by private enterprises). Beijing: Falü chubanshe, 1988.

Fang Sheng. "The Revival of the Individual Economy in Certain Areas." In *China's Economic Reforms*, ed. Lin Wei and Arnold Chao, 172–85.

Feng Lanrui and Zhao Lükuan. "Urban Unemployment in China." *Social Sciences in China* 3, no. 1 (1982): 123–39.

Feuchtwang, Stephen, and Athar Hussain, eds. *The Chinese Economic Reforms*. London: Croom Helm, 1983.

Findlay, Christopher, and Andrew Watson. "Risk and Efficiency: Contracting in the Chinese Countryside." Mimeo, University of Adelaide, February 1989.

Gardner, John. *Chinese Politics and the Succession to Mao*. London and Basingstoke: Macmillan, 1982.

Gold, Thomas. "Guerrilla Interviewing among the Getihu." In *Unofficial China—Popular Culture and Thought in the People's Republic*, ed. Perry Link, 175–92. Boulder, Colo.: Westview Press, 1989.

Grossman, Gregory. "Sub-Rosa Privatization and Marketization in the USSR." *Annals* of the American Academy of Political and Social Science 507 (January 1990): 44–52.

Guo Yongjie. "Zulinzhi de bibing ji duice" (Shortcomings of the leasing system and ways to deal with them). *Jingji yu guanli yanjiu* (Studies in Economics and Management), no. 2 (1987): 37–38.

Guojia gongshang xingzheng guanli ju geti jingji si, eds. *Geti gongshangye guanli zhengce fagui huibian* (Collected laws and regulations on policy toward individual industry and commerce). Beijing: Jingji kexue chubanshe, 1987.

———. *Geti gongshangye jiben qingquang tongji ziliao xuanbian 1949–1986* (Selected statistics on basic conditions in individual industry and commerce, 1949–1986). Internal departmental publication, 1987.

Guojia gongshang xingzheng quanli ju geti jingji si, and *Beijing ribao* lilun bu, eds. *Geti laodongzhe shouce* (Individual laborers' handbook). Beijing: *Beijing ribao* chubanshe and Gongshang chubanshe, 1984.

Guojia gongshang xingzheng guanli ju xinxi zhongxin, eds. *Zhongguo gongshang xingzheng tongji sishi nian* (Forty years of industrial and commercial administration statistics). Beijing: Zhongguo tongji chubanshe, 1992.

Guojia tongji ju, eds. *Zhongguo tongji nianjian* (Statistical Yearbook of China). Beijing: Guojia tongji chubanshe, 1992.

Guowuyuan bangongting diaoyanshi, eds. *Geti jingji diaocha yu yanjiu* (Surveys and research on the individual economy). Beijing: Jingji kexue chubanshe, 1986.

He Jianzhang. "Jiji fuchi, shidang fazhan chengzhen geti jingji" (Actively support and appropriately develop the urban individual economy). *Hongqi* (Red Flag), no. 24 (1981): 13–16.

He Jianzhang and Zhang Wenmin. "The System of Ownership: A Tendency toward Multiplicity." In *China's Economic Reforms*, ed. Lin Wei and Arnold Chao, 186–204.

He Jianzhang and Zhu Qingfang. "Geti jingji de fazhan qishi ji duice—Shenyang shi diaocha de baogao" (Development trends in the individual economy and measures for dealing with them—Shengyang survey report)." Unpublished draft, 1986, provided by the authors. A later version was published in *Gaige zazhi* (Reform magazine), no. 1 (1987).

He Wenfu. "Siying qiye fazhan mianlin de wenti" (Problems concerning the development of private enterprises). *Sichuan jingji yanjiu* (Sichuan Economic Studies), no. 1 (1989): 53–54.

Hershkovitz, Linda. "The Fruits of Ambivalence: China's Urban Individual Economy." *Pacific Affairs* 58, no. 3 (1985): 427–50.

Hu Anchao. "Shilun wo guo siren qiye de falü diwei yu tiaozheng" (A tentative discussion of the legal position and regulation of China's private enterprises). *Nongye jingji wenti* (Problems in Agricultural Economics), no. 11 (1987): 19–21 and 52.

Hu Guohua, Liu Jinghuai, and Chen Min. *Duo sediao de Zhongguo geti jingyingzhe* (The many colors of China's individual business operators). Beijing: Beijing jingji xueyuan chubanshe, 1988.

Huang Chengxi. "Guoying shangye zhudao zuoyong jiantui de yuanyin ji duice" (Causes of the decline in the leading role of state commerce and measures for dealing with it). *FBZ*, F51, no. 10 (1988): 13–16. First published in *Shangye lilun yu shijian* (Commercial Theory and Practice), no. 3 (1988): 37–40.

Huang Jiajing. "Wenzhou de guahu jingying ji qi wanshan wenti" (Wenzhou's *guahu* management and how it can be improved). *Zhejiang xuekan* (Zhejiang Studies), no. 5 (1986): 14–18.

Huang Rutong. "Geti, siying jingji jiankang fazhan zhengce yantaohui guandian zongshu" (Summary of viewpoints at the policy conference on the healthy development of the individual and private economy). *Jingjixue dongtai* (Trends in Economics), no. 11 (1992): 19–23.

Huang Zhongming. "Geti gongshanghu guanli zhong de falü wenti" (Legal problems in individual business administration). *Caijing kexue* (The Science of Finance and Economics), no. 4 (1987): 79–82.

Hunan sheng Anhua xianwei bangongshi diaoyan shi. "Dui zulin jingying zhong jige wenti de tantao" (An inquiry into several problems in leasing management). *Jingji yu guanli yanjiu*, no. 4 (1987): 27–28 and 14.

Ji Jianlin and Zhu Jun. "Siying qiye lirun liuxiang fenxi" (An analysis of profit uses in private enterprises). *Zhongguo nongcun jingji*, no. 9 (1989): 48–52.

Jingji wenti tansuo, eds. *Zhongguo xian jieduan geti jingji yanjiu* (Studies of the individual economy in China's current stage). *Jingji wenti tansuo* (Inquiry into Economic Problems), Supplementary Issue no. 1 (March 1983).

Lardy, Nicholas, and Kenneth Lieberthal, eds. *Chen Yun's Strategy for China's Development*. Armonk, NY: M. E. Sharpe, 1983.

Li Bin and Zhao Ming. "Geti jingji zuoyong de bianhua—Changchun shi chengzhen geti jingji diaocha" (A change in the role of the individual economy—a survey of the urban individual economy in Changchun). *Jingji yanjiu*, no. 3 (1987): 51–53.

Li Chengxun and Zhou Zhixiang, eds. *Zhuanyehu jingying guanli shouce* (Handbook of specialized household management and administration). Beijing: Beijing chubanshe, 1987.

Li Fan, Zhang Xiuwen, Yu Maofa, and Shi Mingzhi. "Shanghai xiao shangpin shichang geti shangfan jingying qingquang yu jiaqiang guanli de yijian" (Operating conditions of individual peddlers in Shanghai's small commodity markets and opinions on improving administration). *Shehui kexue*, no. 9 (1983): 78–80.

Li Jiali. "Geti gongshangye lingdao guanli tizhi jidai gaishan" (The leadership and administration of individual industry and commerce urgently needs improvement). *FBZ*, F51, no. 4 (1987): 42–43. First published in *Jingji gongzuo tongxun* (Economic Work Dispatches), no. 3 (1987): 26–27.

Li Jianjun. "Gugong qiye fazhan bu hui zaocheng liangji fenhua" (The development of employer enterprises will not create polarization). *Jingjixue wenzhai* (Abstracts of Economics), no. 1 (1987): 16–17.

Li Shi. "Wenzhou moshi de jige lilun wenti" (Some theoretical problems of the Wenzhou model). *Jingjixue dongtai* no. 9 (1986): 25–32.

Li Yong and Chen Hongjun. "Geti jingji zai shewai jingji guanxi zhong falü diwei chutan" (A preliminary exploration of the legal position of the individual economy in foreign economic relations). *Faxue zazhi* (Law Journal), no. 4 (1985): 20–21.

Lin, Cyril Chihren (Zhiren). "Open-ended Economic Reform in China." In *Remaking the Economic Institutions of Socialism*, ed. Nee and Stark, 95–136.

———. "The Reinstatement of Economics in China Today." *China Quarterly*, no. 85 (March 1981): 1–48.

Lin Wei and Arnold Chao, eds. *China's Economic Reforms*. Philadelphia: University of Pennsylvania Press, 1982.

Lin Zili, ed. *Shehuizhuyi jingji lun* (Socialist Economics). Vol. 1. Beijing: Jingji kexue chubanshe, 1985.

———. "Wenzhou shangpin jingji de 'chengfen' wenti" (The question of the "class status" of Wenzhou's commodity economy). *RMRB*, 21 November 1986, reprinted in *Xinhua wenzhai*, no. 2 (1987): 36–41.

Liu Guanglu. "Guoying, jiti shangye chuzu guitai qingquang de diaocha" (A survey of conditions in the renting out of counters in state-run and collective commerce). *FBZ*, F51, no. 8 (1989): 113–14. First published in *Liaoning shangye jingji* (Liaoning Commercial Economy), no. 4 (1989): 20–21.

Liu Guoguang. "Guanyu suoyouzhi guanxi gaige de ruogan wenti" (Some problems in the reform of ownership relations). Speech at a conference on the ownership system, 21 November 1985, in *JJRB*, 4 January 1986, p. 3.

———. "Socialism Is Not Egalitarianism." *Beijing Review*, no. 39 (September 28, 1987): 16–18.

Liu Long, ed. *Zhongguo xian jieduan geti jingji yanjiu* (A study of the individual economy in China's current stage). Beijing: Renmin chubanshe, 1986.

Liu Wenpu. "Lun nongcun jiti qiye siyinghua wenti" (On the privatization of management of rural collective enterprises). *NMRB*, 21 September 1988, p. 3, reprinted *FBZ*, F22, no. 10 (1988): 24–25.

Lu, Aiguo, and Mark Selden. "The Reform of Land Ownership and the Political Economy of Contemporary China." *Peasant Studies* 14, no. 4 (Summer 1987): 229–49.

Ma Zheng, Zhou Wei, and Song Heping, eds. *Zhuanyehu getihu zhengce falü guwen* (Advice on policy and law for specialized households and individual businesses). Shenyang: Liaoning daxue chubanshe, 1987.

Marx, Karl. *Capital*. Vol. 1. Moscow: Progress Publishers, 1954. First published in English in 1887.

Muth, Susan Lynn. "Private Business under Socialism: An Examination of the

Urban Individual Economic Sector in China." Ph.D. dissertation, George Washington University, 1987.

Nee, Victor. "Peasant Entrepreneurship and the Politics of Regulation in China." In *Remaking the Economic Institutions of Socialism*, ed. Nee and Stark, 169–207.

Nee, Victor, and David Stark, eds. *Remaking the Economic Institutions of Socialism: China and Eastern Europe*. Stanford: Stanford University Press, 1989.

Nihei, Yuko Akiyoshi. "Unemployment in China: Policies, Problems and Proposals." JETRO *China Newsletter*, no. 38 (May–June 1982): 14–20.

Nove, Alec. *The Economics of Feasible Socialism*. London: George Allen and Unwin, 1983.

Odgaard, Ole. "Collective Control of Income Distribution: A Case Study of Private Enterprises in Sichuan Province." In *Remaking Peasant China*, eds. Jørgen Delman, Stubbe Østergaard, and Flemming Christiansen, 106–21. Aarhus, Denmark: Aarhus University Press, 1990.

———. "The Success of Rural Enterprises in China: Some Notes on Its Social and Economic Effects." *China Information* 3, no. 2 (Autumn 1988): 63–76.

Oi, Jean C., "The Fate of the Collective after the Commune." In *Chinese Society on the Eve of Tiananmen*, eds. Davis and Vogel, 15–36.

———. "Fiscal Reform and the Economic Foundations of Local State Corporatism in China." *World Politics*, no. 45 (October 1992): 99–126.

Pan Zuodi and Xie Jianmin. "Guanyu siren qiye ruogan wenti de tantao" (An exploration of certain questions regarding private enterprises). *Nongye jingji wenti*, no. 1 (1988): 43–45.

Peng Heming. "Yixiang zushi qiye biange de zhongda cuoshi—Chongqing shi zhongqu xiaoxing guoying yinshiye shixing zulin jingying de diaocha" (A major step in promoting enterprise reform—a survey of the implementation of leasing management in small-scale state-run catering in Chongqing). *Caimao jingji* (Finance and Trade Economics), no. 3 (1985): 60–62.

Qian Fenyong. "Fangshou fazhan chengzhen jiti geti jingji" (Boldly develop the urban collective and individual economy). *Shijian* (Practice), no. 4 (1983): 2–4.

Ren Zhonglin. "Guanyu geti jingji wenti" (On the question of the individual economy). Speech at the Central Party school, 7 April 1987. In *Makesi zhuyi lilun jiaoyu cankao ziliao* (Reference materials for Marxist theoretical education), no. 5 (1987): 18–23.

Riskin, Carl. *China's Political Economy—The Quest for Development since 1949*. Oxford and New York: Oxford University Press, 1987.

Rong Jian and Fan Hengshan. "Lun suoyouzhi de kaifang" (On the opening up of the system of ownership). *Xinhua wenzhai*, no. 4 (1989): 36–39.

Shangyebu bangongting, eds. *Shangye zhengce fagui huibian 1983* (Collected laws and regulations on commercial policy, 1983). Beijing: Jingji kexue chubanshe, 1984.

Shi Chenglin. "Dui 'buchong lun' de zai renshi" (A reassessment of the 'supplement theory'). *Nongye jingji wenti*, no. 2 (1989): 15–17.

Shue, Vivienne. *The Reach of the State—Sketches of the Chinese Body Politic*. Stanford: University Press, 1988.

Situ Shuqiang. "Geti jingying yu guoying shangdian jingzheng zhi wo jian" (My view of the competition between individually run and state-run shops). *Guangzhou yanjiu* (Guangzhou Studies), no. 2 (1985): 23.

Siying he geti jingji shiyong fagui daquan (Complete laws and regulations for the private and individual economy). Beijing: Renmin chubanshe, 1988. No editors given.

Solinger, Dorothy J. *Chinese Business under Socialism.* Berkeley: University of California Press, 1984.

―――. "Commerce: The Petty Private Sector and the Three Lines in the Early 1980s." In *Three Visions of Chinese Socialism*, ed. Solinger, 73–111. Boulder, Colo.: Westview Press, 1984.

Song Fangmin and Tan Lansheng. "Lai zi chengshi getihu de tiaozhan" (The challenge of the urban individual businesses). *Xinhua wenzhai* (New China Digest), no. 7 (1985): 56–58.

Sun Ping. "Individual Economy under Socialism." *Beijing Review*, no. 33 (August 13, 1984): 25–30.

Tang Congyao and Xu Youyi, eds. *Zhuanyehu getihu falü zixun shouce* (Handbook of legal advice for specialized households and individual businesses). Tianjin: Zhongguo caizheng jingji chubanshe, 1985.

Tao Youzhi. "Luelun geti jingji de zhengdun yu fazhan" (A brief discussion of the consolidation and development of the individual economy). *Jingji wenti tansuo*, no. 5 (1987): 22–24.

Tong Haosheng and Xu Gang. "You zheyang yi huo nianqing ren" (There is a group of young people like this). *Shijian*, no. 14 (1984): 20–22.

Walder, Andrew. *Communist Neo-Traditionalism—Work and Authority in Chinese Industry.* Berkeley: University of California Press, 1986.

Wang Taixi. "Xi'an shi geti jingji de lishi he xianzhuang" (The history and current situation of Xi'an's individual economy). *Xi'an daxue xuebao* (Xi'an University Journal), no. 4 (1984): 94–101. Reprinted in *FBZ*, F51, no. 12 (1984): 22–29.

Watson, Andrew. "Conflict over Cabbages: The Reform of Wholesale Marketing in China." Hong Kong: Universities Service Centre Seminar Series No. 6, Chinese University of Hong Kong, 1992.

―――. "Investment Issues in the Chinese Countryside." *Australian Journal of Chinese Affairs*, no. 22 (July 1989): 85–126.

―――. "The Management of the Rural Economy: The Institutional Parameters." In *Economic Reform and Social Change in China*, ed. Watson, 171–99. London and New York: Routledge, 1992.

―――. "The Reform of Agricultural Marketing in China since 1978." *China Quarterly*, no. 113 (March 1988): 1–28.

Wu Shangli. "Wo guo geti jingji falü diwei de tantao" (An inquiry into the legal position of China's individual economy). *Caijing kexue*, no. 4 (1987): 75–78.

Xiao Liang. "Guanyu siying jingji de jige lilun wenti" (Several theoretical problems concerning the private economy). *Tianjin shehui kexue* (Social Sciences in Tianjin), no. 4 (1988), extract published in *Xinhua wenzhai*, no. 4 (1988): 44–46.

Xue Mou. "Zenyang zhengque renshi shehuizhuyi gaizao jiben wancheng yihou de xiao shengchan?" (How should we see small production after the basic completion of socialist transformation?) *Hongqi*, no. 21 (1981): 41–43.

Yan Ying'an. "Dui geti keyun jiage yao jiaqiang guanli" (Individual passenger transport prices need more control). *Jiage lilun yu shijian* (Price Theory and Practice), no. 6 (1988): 51.

Yang, Dali L. "Local Government and Rural Industrialization in China." *Peasant Studies* 18, no. 2 (Winter 1991): 131–41.

Yang Xiaokai. "Economic Thinking and Reforms in China." Paper presented at the seminar "Communism's Wake: Some Economic Implications," Centre for Policy Studies, Melbourne, December 1989.

Yang Zhaoxi and Liu Junying. "Zulin shi Beijing xiao shangye mianmao yi xin —Beijing shi guoying shangye xiao qiye shixing zulinzhi gaige de gaikuang" (Leasing gives Beijing's small commerce a new look—an overview of leasing reform in small state-run commercial enterprises in Beijing). *FBZ*, F51, no. 3 (1987): 24–26. Originally published in *Tigai xinxi* (Structural Reform News), no. 4 (1987): 6–8.

You Lianpu. "Lun nongcun jiti qiye siyinghua wenti" (On the privatization of management of rural collective enterprises). *NMRB*, 21 September 1988, p. 3.

———. "Shi lun wo guo xian jieduan siren gugong jingji de xingzhi" (A tentative discussion of the nature of the private employer economy in China's current stage). *Xinhua wenzhai*, no. 11 (1987): 46–48.

Yudkin, Marcia. *Making Good—Private Business in Socialist China.* Beijing: Foreign Languages Press, 1986.

Zhang Caiqing. "Guoying shangye yingdang zhichi geti shangye de shidang fazhan—Jiangsu sheng Wujiang xian geti shangye diaocha" (State-run commerce should support the appropriate development of individual commerce —an investigation into individual commerce in Wujiang county, Jiangsu province). *Caimao jingji*, no. 1 (1984): 58–60 and 57.

Zhang Changyun. "Wo guo xiangzhen qiye suoyouzhi wenti yanjiu" (A study of the ownership system in township enterprises in China). *Nongcun jingji yu shehui* (Rural economy and society), no. 6 (1993): 22–28.

Zhang Houyi and Qin Shaoxiang. "Siying jingji zai dangdai Zhongguo de shijian" (The practice of the private economy in contemporary China). *JJCK*, 14 November, 1988, p. 4.

Zhang Kai. "The Development of Private Enterprises in China." *Shiyue pinglun* (October Review) (June–July 1988): 49–51.

Zhang Renshou, Yang Xiaoguang, and Lin Dayue. " 'Wenzhou moshi' dui jingji tizhi gaige de xiangdao yiyi" (The guiding significance of the "Wenzhou model" for structural economic reform). *Zhejiang xuekan*, no. 5 (1986): 4–10.

Zhao Ziyang. "Yanzhe you Zhongguo tese de shehuizhuyi daolu qianjin" (Advance along the road of socialism with Chinese characteristics). Report to the Thirteenth Congress of the CCP, 25 October 1987, in *JJRB*, 4 November 1987, pp. 1–2.

Zheng Li, Liu Zhaonian, and Xiao Wentong. "Zulin jingying de butong xingshi" (The various forms of leasing management). *Hongqi*, no. 12 (1987): 17–18.

Zheng Xinmiao, Wang Tongxin, and Wu Changling. "Dui nongcun siying jingji fazhan de lilun sikao ji zhengce jianyi" (Theoretical reflections and policy suggestions concerning the development of the rural private economy). *Nongye jingji wenti*, no. 5 (1990): 47–50.

Zhong Dong. "Shehuizhuyi xuyao siyouzhi ma?" (Does socialism need private ownership?). *Guangzhou yanjiu*, no. 5 (1988). Reprinted in *Xinhua wenzhai*, no. 7 (1988): 12–19.

Zhongguo shehui jieji, jieceng yanjiu Guangzhou yanjiu zu. "Guangzhou geti gongshangye, siying qiye jingji zhuangkuang de fenxi" (An analysis of the economic situation in individual industry and commerce and private enterprises in Guangzhou). *Zhongguo wujia* (Prices in China), no. 5 (1990): 42–46.

Zhongguo shehui kexueyuan faxue yanjiusuo, eds. *Zhonghua renmin gongheguo jingji fagui xuanbian, 1982* (Selected economic laws and regulations of the People's Republic of China, 1982). Beijing: Zhongguo caizheng jingji chubanshe, 1983.

Zhongguo shehui kexueyuan nongcun fazhan yanjiusuo siying jingji yanjiuzu. "Wei siying qiye wending, jiankang fazhan chuangzao lianghao de shehui jingji huanjing" (Creating a good socioeconomic environment for the stable and healthy development of private enterprises). *Zhongguo nongcun jingji*, no. 3 (1988): 49–56.

Zhongguo xiangzhen qiye nianjian editorial committee, eds. *Zhongguo xiangzhen qiye nianjian 1993*. Beijing: Nongye chubanshe, 1993.

Index

Susan Young is a visiting fellow at the Centre for East and South-East Asian Studies, University of Copenhagen, where she is pursuing research on ownership and control issues in China's rural enterprises. She formerly taught Chinese language and studies at the University of Adelaide, South Australia, and has made frequent visits to Sichuan, where her fieldwork is based.